Letters of John Adams
Addressed to His Wife

VOLUME 1

EDITED BY
CHARLES FRANCIS ADAMS

CAMBRIDGE
UNIVERSITY PRESS

CAMBRIDGE UNIVERSITY PRESS

Cambridge, New York, Melbourne, Madrid, Cape Town,
Singapore, São Paolo, Delhi, Tokyo, Mexico City

Published in the United States of America by Cambridge University Press, New York

www.cambridge.org
Information on this title: www.cambridge.org/9781108032742

© in this compilation Cambridge University Press 2011

This edition first published 1841
This digitally printed version 2011

ISBN 978-1-108-03274-2 Paperback

CAMBRIDGE LIBRARY COLLECTION

Books of enduring scholarly value

History

The books reissued in this series include accounts of historical events and movements by eye-witnesses and contemporaries, as well as landmark studies that assembled significant source materials or developed new historiographical methods. The series includes work in social, political and military history on a wide range of periods and regions, giving modern scholars ready access to influential publications of the past.

Letters of John Adams Addressed to His Wife

American statesman John Adams (1735–1826) was a key player in the early days of the American Revolution, and the second President of the United States (1797–1801). He was involved in drafting the 1776 Declaration of Independence, and as a Congress representative in Europe negotiated peace with Great Britain. First published in 1841, this two-volume book brings together the letters Adams wrote to his wife Abigail between 1774 and 1801. Spanning twenty-five years crucial to the creation and development of the United States as a nation, these letters reveal Adams' reactions to world events and his political views, as well as his daily life and concern for his family. Edited by Adams' grandson, the letters were largely left in their original form, in order to preserve the vitality and character of Adams' style. Volume 1 covers the early years of Adams' political career, from 1774 to 1777.

Cambridge University Press has long been a pioneer in the reissuing of out-of-print titles from its own backlist, producing digital reprints of books that are still sought after by scholars and students but could not be reprinted economically using traditional technology. The Cambridge Library Collection extends this activity to a wider range of books which are still of importance to researchers and professionals, either for the source material they contain, or as landmarks in the history of their academic discipline.

Drawing from the world-renowned collections in the Cambridge University Library, and guided by the advice of experts in each subject area, Cambridge University Press is using state-of-the-art scanning machines in its own Printing House to capture the content of each book selected for inclusion. The files are processed to give a consistently clear, crisp image, and the books finished to the high quality standard for which the Press is recognised around the world. The latest print-on-demand technology ensures that the books will remain available indefinitely, and that orders for single or multiple copies can quickly be supplied.

The Cambridge Library Collection will bring back to life books of enduring scholarly value (including out-of-copyright works originally issued by other publishers) across a wide range of disciplines in the humanities and social sciences and in science and technology.

LETTERS

OF

JOHN ADAMS.

IN TWO VOLUMES.

John Adams

LETTERS

OF

JOHN ADAMS,

ADDRESSED TO HIS WIFE.

EDITED BY HIS GRANDSON,

CHARLES FRANCIS ADAMS.

VOLUME I.

BOSTON:
CHARLES C. LITTLE AND JAMES BROWN.
MDCCCXLI.

BOSTON:
PRINTED BY FREEMAN AND BOLLES,
WASHINGTON STREET.

PREFACE.

The publication of a number of letters by the wife of John Adams, which had been addressed to him as well as to others, is understood to have excited some curiosity to see his replies. Apart from the general and natural desire to read both parts of any interesting correspondence, a wish has been expressed by some persons to the Editor, that the mode and degree in which the affection and sensibility of the lady were returned should be shown. Intimations have even been made that she has been presented in a favorable light somewhat at the expense of her husband, and that something should be done to restore his reputation as well in his public as in his domestic relations. Although the Editor can scarcely be expected to admit that any apprehensions of this kind are well founded, he knows of no reason why the letters themselves should be withheld from publica-

tion, let the desire to see them proceed from what
motive it may.   Notwithstanding that they
were in their nature private and confidential,
they differ very little in their general character and tone from those papers of Mr. Adams,
which have been long before the world.   As
there was little that was artificial about him
in his life time, there is no danger that his
most secret communications will be at vari-
ance with his declared opinions, or that for
this reason alone it is desirable that anything
should be suppressed.   The volumes now published contain a very full selection from the letters addressed by him to Mrs. Adams, during
the period of twenty-five years, in which long
and frequent separations from her were the
consequence of his public duties.

In submitting these papers to the public, it is
not deemed necessary to prefix any biographi-
cal notice of the writer.   Such a work has been
long expected from far more experienced and
skilful hands than those of the Editor, and may
yet be executed.   The present undertaking is
designed in no way to interfere with that, or to
be other than, perhaps, an incidental aid to its
accomplishment.   As a public man, the leading

events in the life of Mr. Adams are already too
well known to require explanation. But wherever it has been thought that information might
prove useful to the reader, which was not already indirectly supplied by the Memoir of Mrs.
Adams, it has been conveyed in the form of
notes at the foot of the page. Such references
to various historical works, in which the events
and persons here casually mentioned are more
fully described, have been added, as may facili-
tate the researches of the curious. To the labors
of no single individual in this department of
knowledge are they already more indebted than
to those of Professor Sparks. No one who has
ever had occasion to examine the mass of papers
relating to the revolution can fail to appreciate
the extent of patient and minute investigation
that must have been necessary to establish facts
and dates in such a manner that the results
may be relied upon with tolerable certainty by
subsequent generations. The Editor is the
more anxious to acknowledge the great aid he
has derived from this gentleman in the particulars specified, as he finds himself very frequently compelled, whenever the application of
general principles to the facts so carefully de-

tailed is involved, to dissent from the conclu-
sions which he has drawn.

It can scarcely be supposed that the letters
of Mr. Adams will prove quite as attractive to
the public as those of his wife which have been
published, or that they will equally amuse precisely the same class of readers. There is less
of novelty about them and less of that species
of sentiment which appeals at once to the heart
of numbers of both sexes. Yet if it be a recommendation to letters that they are exponents of
personal character, these may be not wholly
without interest. Moreover, the tone and spirit
which run through them will not be found upon
a level at all beneath that which prevails in
Mrs. Adams's productions. Very early in the
period of the Editor's labor a grave question
sprung up for his decision, how far he had a
right to use his judgment in altering or omitting
such portions of these papers as might for various reasons appear to him to be unsuitable for
publication. The difficulty seemed much more
serious in the present case than it had done
in preparing the letters of Mrs. Adams, because
the opinions and acts of Mr. Adams were those
of a leading historical character, and therefore

necessarily bore a more extensive influence upon a much larger circle of cotemporaries than hers could be expected to do. There were some passages which, although well enough when considered as written in the careless way of confidential correspondence, yet looked too trifling for a grave character when publication was in question. Others presented him as holding opinions upon various subjects which clash with the fashionable sentiments of the present day and with the prevailing political dogmas of the sovereign majority in the United States. And still others contain reflections upon individuals which might by possibility and notwithstanding that all the parties have been long removed from the scene, offend the feelings of sensitive descendants or friends. These considerations pressed the Editor very strongly to a thorough revision of the letters, to proceed in which he could feel himself the more justified by the idea that as they had not originally been designed for publication, he should in so doing only be executing what the writer himself would have done if he could have foreseen the use that was now about to be made of them. Yet, however strong these arguments

appeared, obstacles of a very serious character
presented themselves to the performance of the
duty which they recommended. In the first
place, it is a matter of doubt to the Editor how far
any person, by virtue of a self-constituted office,
has a right to alter and modify the language of
another so as to make him appear before the
public as saying more or less than he really
thought. Secondly, admitting such a right to
exist in its full extent, the exercise of it, to any
great degree, appears to be of questionable expediency. For however it may effect the intro-
duction of a tolerable share of uniformity in
literature, this benefit can be gained only at the
expense of all its vitality. The evils attending
it appear to be of two kinds. The first, that it
inevitably makes the character and opinions of
an Editor the standard for judging those of the
writer, and thus confounds all ability to discrim-
inate between them. The second, that it tempts
him to too great subserviency to the popular doctrines of the existing generation at the hazard
of sacrificing what may after all be truth. If
there is one recommendation to a literary work
more than any other to be prized, it is that
it should present the mind of the writer in as

distinct a shape and as free from all extrinsic modeling as possible. The varieties that exist among mankind in temper, disposition principles and affections, are so infinite, that wherever such do not appear in books professing to describe individuals, the inference is almost irresistible that some attempt or other has been made to obliterate those marks by which the difference between them is made visible to all.

Having given to these opposing suggestions all the consideration which they appeared to deserve, the Editor at last determined to adhere closely to the text before him, never varying from it by alteration, and doing so by omission only when the case was of such obvious necessity, from the nature of the subject treated, as to make it an imperative duty. In practising under this rule, the consequences may be, that he has retained many details so trivial that they would have been better omitted, as notices of the weather, of the writer's health, of his children, of his barber, &c. &c., and that he may be thought not to have properly lopped the boldness of expression of which Mr. Adams was often guilty, when, to borrow his own application of the phrase of James Otis, " the zeal pot

boiled over." For errors of judgment, if such
have been committed, his only apology is to be
found in a perhaps over earnest desire to retain
the characteristic features of his author in all
their freshness. At no time of his life was John
Adams a man of many concealments. It would
therefore be strange affectation in any of his
descendants now to strive to make him appear
other than he was or to dilute his strength with
a portion of their weakness. There was no
hypocrisy in him whilst alive and it would
scarcely be doing him justice to invest him
with a share of it after his death. His character and that of his compeers must go down to
be judged by posterity, with whom there is no
chance of the fear or favor that affects the ver-
dicts of cotemporary generations. To that ultimate tribunal the Editor is willing to submit
what evidence passes through his hands without making any puny effort of his own to influence the decision.

The great recommendation of this correspondence, in a historical point of view, is that, as
connected with the period of which it treats,
it is probably unique. Nothing of the same
kind has thus far appeared from any quarter,

much less from persons so actively interested in the management of affairs. The letters of General Washington to his wife were all, with a single trifling exception, destroyed by her a short time before her decease, and her own, if she ever wrote many, probably shared the same fate. Mr. Jefferson lost his wife early, and very little allusion to her is found among his published papers. Other distinguished persons, though of less note, may have written and probably did write letters which would now be very interesting if they had been saved from destruction; but as none such have yet been published, it is to be feared that they have perished. America is not the place for preservation of papers in the hands of families. The modes of life are too migratory, and the means of subsistence too precarious to be favorable to this object. For this reason is it, that the domestic feelings of the revolution are already rapidly eluding the grasp of investigators. The decline of day is the signal for all great objects to throw long shadows, perplexing to just ideas of proportion, and preparatory to a general and dusky twilight. We are beginning to forget that the patriots of former days were men like our-

selves, acting and acted upon like the present
race, and we are almost irresistibly led to ascribe
to them in our imaginations certain gigantic pro-
portions and superhuman qualities, without reflecting that this at once robs their characters of
consistency and their virtues of all merit. It
is imitating the conduct of those poets and ro-
mancers who laud their heroes for courage
after having made them invu.nerable. Fancy
may do what it pleases as its purpose is only to
amuse, but history has a nobler object. The
veneration which attaches to great men should
not be barren of all emulation in those who
feel it. The present race of Americans may
not be called to make precisely the same exertions in the field that were made by their pre-
decessors, but it will be subjected to internal
struggles perhaps even more violent than theirs.
Struggles, success in which makes the glory
that distinguishes the patriot from the dema-
gogue, and the attaining a victory in which
renders the path of rectitude and of honor
equally hard to tread in every age and under
every clime.

The letters of Mr. Adams will be found to
differ in many particulars from those of his wife.

They are generally shorter, more desultory, and
written in more sententious paragraphs. There
is, besides, a spice of humor about them which
is never perceived in hers. Occasionally two
and even three separate sheets of paper were
used on the same day, which might have justified the Editor in regarding them as making
but one letter and moulding them into one form,
had he not preferred exactly to follow the manuscripts. The celebrated letters of the 3d of
July, 1776, have been already treated by some
one else in that manner, and it may be thought
that the effect of them is injured by reëstab-
lishing the shape in which they were originally written. It was not deemed advisable in
that instance to depart from the general rule
which had been applied to all of the unpublished letters. The great object has been to
mark the character of the writer through a me-
dium purely of his own making. This may
take off a little, it is true, from his reputation
of exact prediction in the case in question, but
it has a counterbalancing advantage in restoring the characteristic tone of familiar letters to
what had been made to look a little like studied
declamation. Had Mr. Adams, when address-

ing letters to his wife, been in the practice of formal essay writing, he would doubtless have combined and concentrated his thoughts in a methodical and sustained style. This might have been very good in itself, but would have been out of place when considered as the style of familiar letters. It is the disjointed, irregular chat, now relating the most trivial incidents of common life, and now rising with the subject treated into lofty speculation, yet dwelling long upon nothing, which constitutes their peculiar recommendation. No reader can fail to understand at once, that the writer was in the midst of occupations of a public nature, from which he could only now and then snatch a few moments to give loose to his meditative humor. This must explain the cause why the letters are so short, and why many, which at first sight would appear from their brevity and want of importance scarcely to merit a place in the collection, have been introduced. It is believed that even these will be found to have some bearing upon the general character of the correspondence. For if the object in publishing letters is to place in strong relief the individual who writes them, it surely is of almost as great importance to put in the small traits as the great ones.

It will be perceived that the published correspondence has been carried down to the very last date in the collection, including a considerable number written during the stormy period of twelve years that the federal party was in the ascendant. By inserting these letters, the editor has had no wish or design to awaken animosities or revive party prejudices. He did not hold it at all inconsistent with such a profession to admit many strong expressions of individual sentiment upon the political questions of a period long since passed away, which can have no bearing whatever upon persons or parties in the present day. Mr. Adams's opinions upon government were his own. There was a time when they were much misrepresented for the sake of producing temporary political effects. That time is passed, and no reason now exists why they should not be fairly judged from his own explanations of them. They are not probably much more in unison with the prevailing sentiments in the United States at this time, than when they were first written, but they had been maturely formed, and were sincerely

held, and there is no reason why they should not
be fairly declared. Their ultimate correctness
remains to be tested by experience. Servility to
popular opinion, merely because it was the judgment of the majority, was never the characteristic of Mr. Adams, nor is it the desire of his de-
scendant now to try to build up any fame for him
upon that foundation. The editor has not made
his selection simply upon the ground of inserting
whatever might be perfectly in accordance with
the convictions of others or his own. Such a
principle of action would seem entirely destructive of all individuality of character in families.
His object has been to prepare an amusing, and
it is hoped at the same time, a not wholly un-
instructive compilation, divested of all material
which might be deemed just cause of offence
to any one, and yet retaining a sufficiently
marked character, to fix the attention of general readers. And this has been done, it is
proper to add, solely by himself, upon his own
responsibility, without advice or consultation
with any person.

With these volumes as embracing not all that
could be furnished, but as much as the public
is desirous to see, the editor proposes to finish

his labors. It is, however, due to the descendants of Mrs. Warren, of Plymouth, and of Mrs.
Norton, the niece of Mrs. Adams, to acknowledge their great kindness in furnishing him
with copies of many interesting letters, and
with liberty to use them whenever he should
deem it advisable. It is not his intention to
abuse the indulgent favor, already granted by
the public, in pressing upon them letters to
satiety, or he should have availed himself of
their permission at once.

BOSTON, August, 1841.

CONTENTS.

1777.

LETTERS·

LETTERS.

Boston, 12 May, 1774.

I AM extremely afflicted with the relation your father gave me of the return of your disorder. I fear you have taken some cold. We have had a most pernicious air, a great part of this spring. I am sure I have reason to remember it. My cold is the most obstinate and threatening one I ever had in my life. However I am unwearied in my endeavours to subdue it, and have the pleasure to think I have had some success. I rise at five, walk three miles, keep the air all day and walk again in the afternoon. These walks have done me more good than anything. My own infirmities, the account of the return of yours, and the public news[1] coming altogether have put my utmost philosophy to the trial.

[1] The account of the passage by Parliament of the Boston port bill, of the act for better regulating the government of Massachusetts, and of that to authorize trials to be had in Great

We live, my dear soul, in an age of trial. What will be the consequence, I know not. The town of Boston, for aught I can see, must suffer martyrdom. It must expire. And our principal consolation is, that it dies in a noble cause — the cause of truth, of virtue, of liberty and of humanity, and that it will probably have a glorious resurrection to greater wealth, splendor and power than ever.

Let me know what is best for us to do. It is expensive keeping a family here, and there is no prospect of any business in my way in this town this whole summer. I don't receive a shilling a week. We must contrive as many ways as we can to save expenses; for we may have calls to contribute very largely, in proportion to our circumstances, to prevent other very honest worthy people from suffering for want, besides our own loss in point of business and profit.

Don't imagine from all this that I am in the dumps. Far otherwise. I can truly say, that I have felt more spirits and activity since the arrival of this news than I had done before for years. I look upon this as the last effort of Lord North's despair, and he will as surely be defeated in it, as he was in the project of the tea.

I am, with great anxiety for your health,
Your

JOHN ADAMS.

Britain had just been received. General Gage, who had been appointed Governor with the view to the full execution of these acts, arrived at Boston on the day after the date of this letter.

LETTER II.

York,[1] 29 June, 1774.

MY DEAR,

I HAVE a great deal of leisure, which I chiefly employ in scribbling, that my mind may not stand still or run back, like my fortune. There is very little business here, and David Sewall, David Wyer, John Sullivan and James Sullivan and Theophilus Bradbury are the lawyers who attend the inferior courts, and consequently, conduct the causes at the superior.

I find that the country is the situation to make estates by the law.   John Sullivan, who is placed at Durham in New Hampshire, is younger both in years and practice than I am.   He began with nothing, but is now said to be worth ten thousand pounds lawful money, his brother James allows five or six or perhaps seven thousand pounds, consisting in houses and lands, notes, bonds and mortgages.   He has a fine stream of water with an excellent corn mill, saw mill, fulling mill, scythe mill and others, in all, six mills, which are both his delight and his profit.   As he has earned cash in his business at the bar, he has taken opportunities to purchase farms of his neighbours, who wanted to sell and move out farther into the woods, at an advantageous rate, and in this way has been growing rich ; under the smiles and auspices of Governor

---

[1] Mr. Adams was riding the circuit of the Court according to the practice of lawyers at this time.

Wentworth, he has been promoted in the civil and military way, so that he is treated with great respect in this neighbourhood.

James Sullivan, brother of the other, who studied law under him, without any academical education (and John was in the same case), is fixed at Saco, alias Biddeford, in our province. He began with neither learning, books, estate nor anything but his head and hands, and is now a very popular lawyer and growing rich very fast, purchasing great farms, &c., and a justice of the peace and a member of the General Court.

David Sewall, of this town, never practises out of this county; has no children; has no ambition nor avarice, they say, (however quære.) His business in this county maintains him very handsomely, and he gets beforehand.

Bradbury at Falmouth, they say, grows rich very fast.

I was first sworn in 1758. My life has been a continual scene of fatigue, vexation, labour and anxiety. I have four children. I had a pretty estate from my father; I have been assisted by your father; I have done the greatest business in the province; I have had the very richest clients in the province. Yet I am poor, in comparison with others.

This, I confess, is grievous and discouraging. I ought however to be candid enough to acknowledge that I have been imprudent. I have spent an estate in books; I have spent a sum of money indiscreetly in a lighter, another in a pew, and a much greater in a house in Boston. These would have been indis-

cretions, if the impeachment of the Judges, the Boston port bill, &c. &c., had never happened; but by
the unfortunate interruption of my business from
these causes, those indiscretions became almost fatal
to me ; to be sure, much more detrimental.

John Lowell, at Newburyport, has built himself a
house like the palace of a nobleman, and lives in
great splendor. His business is very profitable. In
short, every lawyer who has the least appearance of
abilities, makes it do in the country. In town, nobody
does, or ever can, who either is not obstinately determined never to have any connexion with politics, or
does not engage on the side of the Government, the
Administration and the Court.

Let us, therefore, my dear partner, from that affection which we feel for our lovely babes, apply ourselves, by every way we can, to the cultivation of our
farm. Let frugality and industry be our virtues, if
they are not of any others. And above all cares of
this life, let our ardent anxiety be, to mould the minds
and manners of our children. Let us teach them not
only to do virtuously, but to excel. To excel, they
must be taught to be steady, active and industrious.

  I am, &c.   Your
         JOHN ADAMS.

LETTER III.

Falmouth,[1] 6 July, 1774.

MOBS are the trite topic of declamation and in-
vective among all the ministerial people far and near.
They are grown universally learned in the nature,
tendency and consequences of them, and very elegant and pathetic in descanting upon them. They
are sources of all kinds of evils, vices and crimes, they
say. They give rise to profaneness, intemperance,
thefts, robberies, murders, and treason. Cursing,
swearing, drunkenness, gluttony, lewdness, trespasses,
maims are necessarily involved in them and occasioned by them. Besides, they render the populace, the
rabble, the scum of the earth, insolent and disorderly,
impudent and abusive. They give rise to lying,
hypocrisy, chicanery and even perjury among the
people, who are driven to such artifices and crimes,
to conceal themselves and their companions from
prosecutions in consequence of them.

This is the picture drawn by the Tory pencil;
and it must be granted to be a likeness. But this is
declamation. What consequence is to be drawn from
this description? Shall we submit to parliamentary
taxation, to avoid mobs? Will not parliamentary
taxation, if established, occasion vices, crimes and
follies, infinitely more numerous, dangerous and

[1] The ancient name of Portland, in the State of Maine, at
this period a part of the province of Massachusetts Bay.

fatal to the community? Will not parliamentary taxation, if established, raise a revenue unjustly and wrongfully? If this revenue is scattered by the hand of corruption among the public officers and magistrates and rulers in the community, will it not propagate vices more numerous, more malignant and pestilential among them? Will it not render magistrates servile and fawning to their vicious superiors, and insolent and tyrannical to their inferiors? Are insolence, abuse and impudence, more tolerable in a magistrate than in a subject? Are they not more constantly and extensively pernicious? And does not the example of vice and folly in magistrates descend and spread downwards among the people?

Besides, is not the insolence of officers, and soldiers, and seamen, in the army and navy, as mischievous as that of porters, or of sailors in the merchant service? Are not riots, raised and made by armed men, as bad, as those by unarmed? Is not an assault upon a civil officer, and a rescue of a prisoner from lawful authority, made by soldiers with swords or bayonets, as bad, as if made by tradesmen with staves?

Are not the killing of a child by R.,[1] and the slaughter of half a dozen citizens by a party of soldiers, as bad as pulling down a house or drowning a cargo of

[1] Ebenezer Richardson, who fired upon a mob, and killed Christopher Snider, a boy eleven years old. The account is given by Hutchinson, vol. 3, p. 269, and Gordon, vol. 1, p. 276. The other allusion is to what was called the Boston Massacre.

tea, even if both should be allowed to be unlawful ?
Parties may go on declaiming, but it is not easy to
say, which party has excited most riots, which has
published most libels, which has propagated most
slander, and defamation ? Verbal scandal has been
propagated in great abundance by both parties ; but
there is this difference, that one party have enjoyed
almost all public offices, and therefore, their defamation has been spread among the people more secretly,
more maliciously and more effectually. It has gone
with greater authority, and been scattered by instru-
ments more industrious. The ministerial newspapers have swarmed with as numerous and as malicious libels as the antiministerial ones. Fleet's paper, Mein's Chronicle, &c. &c., have been as virulent as
any that was ever in the province. These bickerings
of opposite parties, and their mutual reproaches, their
declamations, their sing-song, their triumphs and de-
fiances, their dismals and prophecies are all delusion.

We very seldom hear any solid reasoning. I
wish always to discuss the question, without all painting, pathos, rhetoric or flourish of every kind. And
the question seems to me to be, whether the American colonies are to be considered as a distinct community so far as to have a right to judge for themselves, when the fundamentals of their government
are destroyed or invaded ? or whether they are to be
considered as a part of the whole British empire,
the whole English nation, so far as to be bound in
honor, conscience or interest by the general sense

of the whole nation ?   However, if this was the rule, I believe it is very far from the general sense of the whole nation, that America should be taxed by the British parliament.   If the sense of the whole of the Empire could be fairly and truly collected, it would appear, I believe, that a great majority would be against taxing us, against or without our consent.   It is very certain, that the sense of parliament is not the sense of the empire, nor a sure indication of it.

But, if all other parts of the empire were agreed unanimously in the propriety and rectitude of taxing us, this would not bind us.   It is a fundamental, inherent and unalienable right of the people, that they have some check, influence or control in their supreme legislature.   If the right of taxation is conceded to parliament, the Americans have no check or influence at all left.   This reasoning never was nor can be answered.

JOHN ADAMS.

LETTER IV.

Falmouth, 7 July, 1774.

MY DEAR,

HAVE you seen a list of the addressers of the late Governor ?   There is one abroad, with the character, profession or occupation of each person against his name.   I have never seen it, but Judge Brown says,

against the name of Andrew Faneuil Phillips is
" Nothing." And that Andrew, when he first heard
of it, said : " Better be nothing with one side, than
every thing with the other." This was witty and
smart, whether Andrew said it, or, what is more likely,
it was made for him. A notion prevails among all
parties, that it is politest and genteelest to be on the
side of Administration ; that the better sort, the
wiser few are on one side ; and that the multitude,
the vulgar, the herd, the rabble, the mob only are on
the other. So difficult it is for the frail, feeble mind
of man to shake itself loose from all prejudice and
habits. However Andrew or his prompter is perfectly right in his judgment, and will finally be proved to
be so, that the lowest on the Tory scale will make it
more for his interest than the highest on the Whig-
gish. And as long as a man adheres immovably to
his own interest, and has understanding or luck enough
to secure and promote it, he will have the character
of a man of sense, and will be respected by a selfish
world. I know of no better reason for it than this,
that most men are conscious that they aim at their
own interest only, and that if they fail, it is owing to
short sight or ill luck, and therefore they can 't blame,
but secretly applaud, admire and sometimes envy those,
whose capacities have proved greater and fortunes
more prosperous.

I am engaged in a famous cause. The cause of
King of Scarborough *versus* a mob that broke into his
house and rifled his papers and terrified him, his wife,
children and servants in the night. The terror and

distress, the distraction and horror of this family cannot be described by words, or painted upon canvass.
It is enough to move a statue, to melt a heart of stone,
to read the story. A mind susceptible of the feelings
of humanity, a heart which can be touched with sensibility for human misery and wretchedness must re-
luct, must burn with resentment and indignation at
such outrageous injuries. These private mobs I do
and will detest. If popular commotions can be justified in opposition to attacks upon the Constitution, it
can be only, when fundamentals are invaded, nor then,
unless for absolute necessity, and with great caution.
But these tarrings and featherings, this breaking open
houses by rude and insolent rabble in resentment for
private wrongs, or in pursuance of private prejudices
and passions, must be discountenanced. It cannot be
even excused upon any principle, which can be entertained by a good citizen, a worthy member of society.

Dined with Mr. Collector Francis Waldo, Esquire, in
company with Mr. Winthrop, the two Quincys and
the two Sullivans, all very social and cheerful —
full of politics. S. Quincy's tongue ran as fast as
any body's. He was clear in it, that the House of
Commons had no right to take money out of our
pockets more than any foreign state ; repeated
large paragraphs from a publication of Mr. Burke's
in 1766, and large paragraphs from Junius America-
nus, &c. This is to talk and to shine before persons
who have no capacity of judging, and who do not
know, that he is ignorant of every rope in the ship.

I shan 't be able to get away till next week. I am concerned only in two or three cases, and none of them are come on yet. Such an Eastern circuit I never made. I shall bring home as much as I brought from home, I hope, and not much more, I fear. I go mourning in my heart all the day long, though I say nothing. I am melancholy for the public and anxious for my family. As for myself, a frock and trowsers, a hoe and a spade would do for my remaining days.

For God's sake make your children *hardy*, *active*, and *industrious;* for strength, activity and industry will be their only resource and dependence.

JOHN ADAMS.

<hr />

LETTER V.

Falmouth, 9 July, 1774.

MY DEAR,

I NEVER enjoyed better health in any of my journeys, but this has been the most tedious, the most irksome, the most gloomy and melancholy I ever made. I cannot, with all my philosophy and christian resignation, keep up my spirits. The dismal prospect before me, my family, and my country, is too much for my fortitude.

> " Bear me, some God ! Oh quickly bear me hence
> To wholesome solitude, the nurse of sense ;
> Where contemplation prunes her ruffled wings,
> And the free soul looks down to pity kings."

The day before yesterday, a gentleman came and spoke to me, asked me to dine with him on Saturday; said he was very sorry I had not better lodgings in town; desired, if I came to town again, I would take a bed at his house and make his house my home, I should always be very welcome. I told him I had not the pleasure of knowing him. He said his name was Codman. I said I was very much obliged to him, but I was very well accommodated where I lodged. I had a clean bed and a very neat house, a chamber to myself, and every thing I wanted.

Saturday, I dined with him, in company with Brigadier Preble, Major Freeman and his son, &c., and a very genteel dinner we had. Salt fish and all its apparatus, roast chickens, bacon, peas, as fine a salad as ever was made, and a rich meat pie. Tarts and custards, &c., good wine and as good punch as ever you made. A large, spacious, elegant house, yard and garden; I thought I had got into the palace of a nobleman. After dinner, when I was obliged to come away, he renewed his invitation to me, to make his house my home whenever I shall come to town again.

Friday, I dined with Colonel, Sheriff, alias Bill Tyng. Mrs. Ross and her daughter Mrs. Tyng dined with us, and the Court, and Clerk, and some of the bar. At table, we were speaking about Captain MacCarty, which led to the African trade. Judge Trowbridge said, " That was a very humane and christian trade, to be sure, that of making slaves." " Ay," says I, " it makes no great odds; it is a trade that almost all mankind have been concerned in, all over the globe, since Adam, more or less, in one way and another." This occasioned a laugh.

At another time, Judge Trowbridge said, " It seems, by Colonel Barre's speeches, that Mr. Otis has acquired honor by releasing his damages to Robinson." "Yes," says I, " he has acquired honor with all generations." Trowbridge. " He did not make much profit, I think." Adams. " True, but the less profit, the more honor. He was a man of honor and generosity, and those who think he was mistaken, will pity him."

Thus you see how foolish I am. I cannot avoid exposing myself before these high folks; my feelings will at times overcome my modesty and reserve, my prudence, policy and discretion. I have a zeal at my heart for my country and her friends, which I cannot smother or conceal; it will burn out at times and in companies, where it ought to be latent in my breast. This zeal will prove fatal to the fortune and felicity of my family, if it is not regulated by a cooler judgment than mine has hitherto been. Colonel Otis's phrase is, " The zeal-pot boils over."

I am to wait upon brother Bradbury to meeting to-day, and to dine with brother Wyer. When I shall get home, I know not, but if possible, it shall be before next Saturday night. I long for that time to come, when my dear wife and my charming little prattlers will embrace me.

                                   Your
                                           JOHN ADAMS.

LETTER VI.

Princeton, New Jersey, 23 August, 1774.

I RECEIVED your kind letter[1] at New York, and it is not easy for you to imagine the pleasure it has given me. I have not found a single opportunity to write since I left Boston, excepting by the post, and I don't choose to write by that conveyance, for fear of foul play. But as we are now within forty-two miles of Philadelphia, I hope there to find some private hand by which I can convey this.

The particulars of our journey I must reserve, to be communicated after my return. It would take a volume to describe the whole. It has been upon the whole an agreeable jaunt. We have had opportunities to see the world and to form acquaintances with the most eminent and famous men, in the several Colonies we have passed through. We have been treated with unbounded civility, complaisance and respect. We yesterday visited Nassau Hall College, and were politely treated by the scholars, tutors, professors, and President whom we are this day to hear preach. Tomorrow we reach the theatre of action.[2] God Almighty grant us wisdom and virtue sufficient

---

[1] See this letter among those of Mrs. Adams, 19 August, 1774. Vol. I. p. 13.

[2] Mr. Adams was on his way to attend the meeting of the first Congress at Philadelphia.

for the high trust that is devolved upon us.   The spirit
of the people, wherever we have been, seems to be
very favorable.   They universally consider our cause
as their own, and express the firmest resolution to
abide by the determination of the Congress.

I am anxious for our perplexed, distressed province ;
hope they will be directed into the right path.   Let
me entreat you, my dear, to make yourself as easy
and quiet as possible.   Resignation to the will of
Heaven is our only resource in such dangerous times.
Prudence and caution should be our guides.   I have
the strongest hopes that we shall yet see a clearer
sky and better times.

Remember my tender love to little Abby — tell her
she must write me a letter and inclose it in the next
you send.   I am charmed with your amusement with
our little Johnny.   Tell him I am glad to hear he is
so good a boy as to read to his mamma for her entertainment, and to keep himself out of the company of
rude children.   Tell him I hope to hear a good account of his accidence and nomenclature when I return.   Remember me to all inquiring friends, particularly to uncle Quincy, your papa and family, and
Dr. Tufts and family.   Mr. Thaxter, I hope, is a
good companion, in your solitude.   Tell him, if he
devotes his soul and body to his books, I hope, notwithstanding the darkness of these days, he will not
find them unprofitable sacrifices in future.   I have
received three very obliging letters from Tudor,
Trumbull and Hill.   They have cheered us in our
wanderings and done us much service.

Your account of the rain refreshed me. I hope our husbandry is prudently and industriously managed. Frugality must be our support. Our expenses in this journey will be very great. Our only [recompense will [1]] be the consolatory reflection that we toil, spend our time and [encounter] dangers for the public good — happy indeed if we do any good.

The education of our children is never out of my mind. Train them to virtue. Habituate them to industry, activity and spirit. Make them consider every vice as shameful and unmanly. Fire them with ambition to be useful. Make them disdain to be destitute of any useful or ornamental knowledge or accomplishment. Fix their ambition upon great and solid objects, and their contempt upon little, frivolous and useless ones. It is time, my dear, for you to begin to teach them French. Every decency, grace and honesty should be inculcated upon them.

I have kept a few minutes by way of journal, which shall be your entertainment when I come home ; but we have had so many persons and so various characters to converse with, and so many objects to view, that I have not been able to be so particular as I could wish. I am, with the tenderest affection and concern,

Your wandering

JOHN ADAMS.

---

[1] The words inclosed within brackets have been supplied, the manuscript being defective in those places.

LETTER VII.

Philadelphia, 8 September, 1774.

MY DEAR,

WHEN or where this letter will find you, I know not. In what scenes of distress and terror, I cannot fore-see. We have received a confused account from Boston of a dreadful catastrophe. The particulars we have not heard. We are waiting with the utmost anxiety and impatience, for further intelligence. The effect of the news we have, both upon the Congress and the inhabitants of this city, was very great. Great indeed! Every gentleman seems to consider the bombardment[1] of Boston as the bombardment of the capital of his own province. Our deliberations are grave and serious indeed.

It is a great affliction to me that I cannot write to you oftener than I do. But there are so many hindrances, that I cannot. It would fill volumes, to give you an idea of the scenes I behold, and the characters I converse with. We have so much business, so much ceremony, so much company, so many visits to receive and return, that I have not time to write. And the times are such as to make it impru-dent to write freely.

---

[1] A rumor of this kind had been spread, occasioned by the military preparations, made by General Gage around the town, to guard against surprise.

We cannot depart from this place until the business of the Congress is completed, and it is the general disposition to proceed slowly. When I shall be at home I can't say. If there is distress and danger in Boston, pray invite our friends, as many as possible, to take an asylum with you — Mrs. Cushing and Mrs. Adams, if you can. There is in the Congress a collection of the greatest men upon this continent in point of abilities, virtues, and fortunes. The magnanimity and public spirit which I see here make me blush for the sordid, venal herd which I have seen in my own Province. The Addressers, and the new Councillors,[1] are held in universal contempt and abhorrence from one end of the continent to the other.

Be not under any concern for me. There is little danger from any thing we shall do at the Congress. There is such a spirit through the colonies, and the members of the Congress are such characters, that no danger can happen to us, which will not involve the whole continent in universal desolation; and in that case, who would wish to live?

Adieu.

JOHN ADAMS.

---

[1] Persons who accepted seats as councillors, by virtue of a mandamus from the king. The Addressers were those who signed an address to Governor Hutchinson, on his departure.

LETTER VIII.

Philadelphia, 14 September, 1774.

MY DEAR,

I HAVE written but once to you since I left you. This is to be imputed to a variety of causes, which I cannot explain for want of time. It would fill volumes to give you an exact idea of the whole tour. My time is totally filled from the moment I get out of bed until I return to it. Visits, ceremonies, company, business, newspapers, pamphlets, &c. &c. &c.

The Congress will, to all present appearance, be well united, and in such measures as, I hope, will give satisfaction to the friends of our country. A Tory here is the most despicable animal in the creation. Spiders, toads, snakes are their only proper emblems. The Massachusetts Councillors and Addressers are held in curious esteem here, as you will see. The spirit, the firmness, the prudence of our province are vastly applauded, and we are universally acknowledged, the saviours and defenders of American liberty. The designs and plans of the Congress must not be communicated until completed, and we shall move with great deliberation.

When I shall come home I know not, but at present, I do not expect to take my leave of this city these four weeks. My compliments, love, service, where they are due. My babes are never out of my mind, nor absent from my heart.

Adieu.   JOHN ADAMS.

LETTER IX.

Philadelphia, 16 September, 1774.

HAVING a leisure moment, while the Congress is assembling, I gladly embrace it to write you a line.

When the Congress first met, Mr. Cushing made a motion that it should be opened with prayer. It was opposed by Mr. Jay of New York and Mr. Rutledge of South Carolina, because we were so divided in religious sentiments; some Episcopalians, some Quakers, some Anabaptists, some Presbyterians, and some Congregationalists, that we could not join in the same act of worship. Mr. Samuel Adams arose and said, "he was no bigot, and could hear a prayer from a gentleman of piety and virtue, who was at the same time a friend to his country. He was a stranger in Philadelphia, but had heard that Mr. Duché" (Dushay they pronounce it) "deserved that character, and therefore he moved, that Mr. Duché, an episcopal clergyman, might be desired to read prayers to the Congress tomorrow morning." The motion was seconded and passed in the affirmative. Mr. Randolph, our President, waited on Mr. Duché and received for answer that, if his health would permit, he certainly would. Accordingly, next morning he appeared with his clerk and in his pontificals, and read several prayers in the established form, and then read the collect for the seventh day of September, which was the thirty-fifth Psalm. You must remember, this was the next morning after we heard the horrible rumor of the cannonade of Boston. I never saw a greater effect upon an audience. It seemed as if Heaven had ordained that Psalm to be read on that morning.

After this, Mr. Duché, unexpectedly to every body, struck out into an extemporary prayer, which filled the bosom of every man present. I must confess, I never heard a better prayer, or one so well pronounced. Episcopalian as he is, Dr. Cooper himself never prayed with such fervor, such ardor, such earnestness and pathos, and in language so elegant and sublime, for America, for the Congress, for the province of Massachusetts Bay, and especially the town of Boston. It has had an excellent effect upon every body here. I must beg you to read that Psalm. If there was any faith in the sortes Virgilianæ, or sortes Homericæ, or especially the sortes Biblicæ, it would be thought providential.

It will amuse your friends to read this letter and the 35th Psalm to them. Read it to your father and Mr. Wibird. I wonder what our Braintree churchmen would think of this. Mr. Duché is one of the most ingenious men, and best characters, and greatest orators in the episcopal order upon this continent; yet a zealous friend of liberty and his country.

I long to see my dear family — God bless, preserve, and prosper it.

Adieu.

JOHN ADAMS.

LETTER X.

Philadelphia, 18 September, 1774.

MY DEAR,

I RECEIVED your very agreeable letter by Mr. Mars-
ton, and have received two others which gave me
much pleasure. I have written several letters, but
whether they have reached you, I know not. There
is so much rascality in the management of letters now
come in fashion, that I am determined to write nothing of consequence, not even to the friend of my bosom, but by conveyances which I can be sure of.

The proceedings of the Congress are all a profound
secret as yet, except two votes which were passed
yesterday, and ordered to be printed. You will see
them from every quarter. These votes[1] were passed
in full Congress with perfect unanimity. The esteem,
the affection, the admiration for the people of Boston
and the Massachusetts, which were expressed yesterday, and the fixed determination that they should
be supported, were enough to melt a heart of stone.
I saw the tears gush into the eyes of the old, grave,
pacific Quakers of Pennsylvania.

You cannot conceive, my dear, the hurry of business, visits, and ceremonies which we are obliged to
go through.

We have a delicate course to steer between too

---

[1] These resolutions will be found in the journals of the first
Congress for Saturday, 17 September, 1774.

much activity, and too much insensibility in our critical, interested situation.   I flatter myself, however,
that we shall conduct our embassy in such a manner,
as to merit the approbation of our country.   It has
taken us much time to get acquainted with the tempers, views, characters and designs of persons, and to
let them into the circumstances of our province.   My
dear, do intreat every friend I have to write me.
Every line which comes from our friends is greedily
inquired after, and our letters have done us vast service.   Middlesex and Suffolk have acquired unbounded honor here.   There is no idea of submission here
in anybody's head.

Thank my dear Abby for her letter; tell her it
has given me great spirits.   Kiss all my sweet ones
for me.

Adieu.

JOHN ADAMS.

LETTER XI.

Philadelphia, 18 September, 1774.

MY DEAR,

IN your last,[1] you inquire tenderly after my health,
and how we found the people upon our journey, and

---

[1] See Mrs. Adams's letter, dated 2 September, 1774, Vol.
I. p. 15.

how we were treated. I have enjoyed as good health as usual, and much more than I know how to account for, when I consider the extreme heat of the weather, and the incessant feasting I have endured ever since I left Boston.

The people in Connecticut, New York, the Jerseys, and Pennsylvania, we have found extremely well principled, and very well inclined, although some persons in New York and Philadelphia wanted a little animation. Their zeal, however, has increased wonderfully since we began our journey. When the horrid news was brought here of the bombardment of Boston, which made us completely miserable for two days, we saw proofs both of the sympathy and the resolution of the continent. War! war! war! was the cry, and it was pronounced in a tone which would have done honor to the oratory of a Briton or a Roman. If it had proved true, you would have heard the thunder of an American Congress.

I have not time, nor language to express the hospitality and the studied and expensive respect with which we have been treated in every stage of our progress. If Camden, Chatham, Richmond and St. Asaph had travelled through the country, they could not have been entertained with greater demonstrations of respect than Cushing, Paine, and the brace of Adamses have been. The particulars will amuse you when we return.

I confess, the kindness, the affection, the applause which have been given to me, and especially to our province, have many a time filled my bosom and streamed from my eyes.

My best respects to Colonel Warren and his lady when you write to them. I wish to write them.

Adieu.

JOHN ADAMS.

———

LETTER XII.

Philadelphia, 20 September, 1774.

MY DEAR,

I AM very well yet. Write to me as often as you can, and send your letters to the office in Boston, or to Mr. Cranch's, whence they will be sent by the first conveyance.

I am anxious to know how you can live without government. But the experiment must be tried. The evils will not be found so dreadful as you apprehend them. Frugality, my dear, frugality, economy, parsimony, must be our refuge. I hope the ladies are every day diminishing their ornaments, and the gentlemen too. Let us eat potatoes, and drink water. Let us wear canvass, and undressed sheepskins, rather than submit to the unrighteous, and ignominious domination that is prepared for us.

Tell Brackett I shall make him leave off drinking rum. We can't let him fight yet. My love to my dear ones.

Adieu.

JOHN ADAMS.

LETTER XIII.

Philadelphia, 25 September, 1774.

MY DEAR,

I would not lose the opportunity of writing to you, though I must be short.

Tedious indeed is our business — slow as snails. I have not been used to such ways. We sit only before dinner. We dine at four o'clock. We are crowded with a levee in the evening.

Fifty gentlemen meeting together, all strangers, are not acquainted with each other's language, ideas, views, designs. They are therefore jealous of each other — fearful, timid, skittish.[1]

LETTER XIV.

Philadelphia, 29 September, 1774.

MY DEAR,

SITTING down to write you is a scene almost too tender for my state of nerves.

It calls up to my view the anxious, distressed state you must be in, amidst the confusion and dangers which surround you. I long to return and

----

[1] Without signature, which is often the case.

administer all the consolation in my power, but when
I shall have accomplished all the business I have
to do here, I know not, and if it should be necessary to stay here till Christmas, or longer, in order
to effect our purposes, I am determined patiently to
wait.

Patience, forbearance, long suffering are the lessons taught here for our province, and at the same
time, absolute and open resistance to the new Government. I wish I could convince gentlemen of the
danger, or impracticability of this as fully as I believe it myself. The art and address of ambassadors
from a dozen belligerent powers of Europe ; nay, of
a conclave of cardinals at the election of a pope ;
or of the princes in Germany at the choice of an
Emperor, would not exceed the specimens we have
seen ; yet the Congress all profess the same political
principles. They all profess to consider our province,
as suffering in the common cause, and indeed they
seem to feel for us, as if for themselves. We have
had as great questions to discuss as ever engaged the
attention of men, and an infinite multitude of them.

I received a very kind letter from Deacon Palmer,
acquainting me with Mr. Cranch's designs of removing to Braintree, which I approve very much, and
wish I had a house for every family in Boston, and
abilities to provide for them in the country. I submit it to you, my dear, whether it would not be best
to remove all the books, and papers, and furniture in
the Office at Boston up to Braintree. There will
be no business there, nor any where, I suppose, and

my young friends can study there better than in Boston at present.

I shall be killed with kindness in this place. We go to Congress at nine, and there we stay, most earnestly engaged in debates upon the most abstruse mysteries of state, until three in the afternoon ; then we adjourn, and go to dine with some of the nobles of Pennsylvania at four o'clock, and feast upon ten thousand delicacies, and sit drinking Madeira, Claret and Burgundy till six or seven, and then go home fatigued to death with business, company, and care. Yet I hold it out surprisingly.

Yours, most affectionately,
JOHN ADAMS.

LETTER XV.

Philadelphia, 7 October, 1774.

MY DEAR,

I THANK you for all your kind favors. I wish I could write to you much oftener than I do. I wish I could write to you a dozen letters every day. But the business before me is so arduous, and takes up my time so entirely, that I cannot write often. I had the characters and tempers, the principles and views of fifty gentlemen, total strangers to me, to study, and the trade, policy, and whole interest of a dozen provinces to learn, when I came here. I have multitudes

of pamphlets, newspapers, and private letters to read.
I have numberless plans of policy and many arguments to consider. I have many visits to make and
receive, much ceremony to endure, which cannot
be avoided, which, you know, I hate.

There is a great spirit in the Congress. But our people must be peaceable. Let them exercise every day
in the week, if they will; the more, the better.
Let them furnish themselves with artillery, arms, and
ammunition. Let them follow the maxim, which you
say they have adopted, " In times of peace prepare
for war." But let them avoid war *if possible* — *if
possible*, I say.

Mr. Revere, will bring you the doings of the Congress, who are now all around me, debating what advice to give to Boston and the Massachusetts Bay.

We are all well — hope our family is so. Remember me to them all. I have advised you before,
to remove my Office from Boston to Braintree. It is
now, I think, absolutely necessary. Let the best care
be taken of all books and papers. Tell all my clerks
to mind their books and study hard, for their country
will stand in need of able counsellors. I must give you
a general license to make my compliments to all my
friends, and acquaintances. I have not time to name
them particularly. I wish they would all write to me.
If they leave letters at Edes and Gill's, they will soon
be sent to me.

I long to be at home, but I cannot say when. I
will never leave the Congress until it rises, and when
it will rise, I cannot say. And indeed I cannot say

but we are better here than any where. We have fine opportunities here to serve Boston and Massachusetts, by acquainting the whole continent with the true state of them. Our residence here greatly serves the cause. The spirit and principles of liberty here are greatly cherished by our presence and conversation. The elections of last week prove this. Mr. Dickinson was chosen, almost unanimously, a representative of the county. The broad-brims began an opposition to your friend Mr. Mifflin, because he was too warm in the cause. This instantly alarmed the friends of liberty, and ended in the election of Mr. Mifflin by eleven hundred votes out of thirteen, and in the election of our Secretary, Mr. Charles Thomson, to be a burgess with him. This is considered here as a most complete and decisive victory in favor of the American cause. And, it is said, it will change the balance in the Legislature here against Mr. Galloway, who has been supposed to sit on the skirts of the American advocates.

Mrs. Mifflin, who is a charming Quaker girl, often inquires kindly after your health.

Adieu, my dear wife. God bless you and yours; so wishes and prays, without ceasing,

JOHN ADAMS.

LETTER XVI.

Philadelphia, 9 October, 1774.

MY DEAR,

I AM wearied to death with the life I lead. The business of the Congress is tedious beyond expression. This assembly is like no other that ever existed. Every man in it is a great man, an orator, a critic, a statesman ; and therefore, every man upon every question, must show his oratory, his criticism, and his political abilities. The consequence of this is, that business is drawn and spun out to an immeasurable length. I believe, if it was moved and seconded, that we should come to a resolution that three and two make five, we should be entertained with logic, and rhetoric, law, history, politics and mathematics, and then — we should pass the resolution, unanimously, in the affirmative. The perpetual round of feasting too, which we are obliged to submit to, makes the pilgrimage more tedious to me.

This day, I went to Dr. Allison's meeting in the forenoon, and heard the Dr. ; a good discourse upon the Lord's supper. This is a Presbyterian meeting. I confess I am not fond of the Presbyterian meetings in this town. I had rather go to church. We have better sermons, better prayers, better speakers, softer, sweeter music, and genteeler company. And I must confess, that the Episcopal church is quite as agreeable to my taste as the Presbyterian. They are both slaves to the domination of the priesthood. I like the Congregational way best ; next to that, the Independent.

This afternoon, led by a curiosity and good company, I strolled away to mother church, or rather, grandmother church. I mean the Romish Chapel. I heard a good, short, moral essay upon the duty of parents to their children founded in justice and charity, to take care of their interests, temporal and spiritual. This afternoon's entertainment was to me most awful and affecting. The poor wretches fingering their beads, chanting Latin, not a word of which they understood ; their pater nosters and ave Marias ; their holy water ; their crossing themselves perpetually ; their bowing to the name of Jesus, wherever they hear it ; their bowings, and kneelings, and genuflections before the altar. The dress of the priest was rich with lace. His pulpit was velvet and gold. The altar-piece was very rich ; little images and crucifixes about ; wax candles lighted up. But how shall I describe the picture of our Saviour, in a frame of marble over the altar, at full length, upon the cross in the agonies, and the blood dropping and streaming from his wounds ! The music, consisting of an organ and a choir of singers, went all the afternoon, except sermon time. And the assembly chanted most sweetly and exquisitely.

Here is everything which can lay hold of the eye, ear, and imagination. Everything which can charm, and bewitch the simple and ignorant. I wonder how Luther ever broke the spell.

Adieu. JOHN ADAMS.

LETTER XVII.

Hartford,[1] 30 April, 1775.

New York has appointed an ample representation in our Congress, and has appointed a provincial Congress. The people of the city have seized the city arms and ammunition out of the hands of the Mayor, who is a creature of the Governor. Lord North will certainly be disappointed in his expectation of seducing New York. The tories there durst not show their heads. The Jerseys are aroused, and greatly assist the friends of liberty in New York. North Carolina has done bravely; chosen the old delegates in provincial Congress, and then confirmed the choice in general assembly, in opposition to all that Governor Martin could do. The assembly of this colony is now sitting at Hartford. We are treated with great tenderness, sympathy, friendship, and respect. Every thing is doing by this colony that can be done by men, both for New York and Boston. Keep your spirits composed and calm, and don't suffer yourself to be disturbed by idle reports and frivolous alarms. We shall see better times yet. Lord North is ensuring us success. I am wounded to the heart with the news, this moment told me, of Josiah Quincy's death.

---

[1] Mr. Adams was now again on the road to Philadelphia, to attend the second session of the Congress.

LETTER XVIII.

Hartford, 2 May, 1775.

Our hearts are bleeding for the poor people of Boston. What will or can be done for them, I can't conceive. God preserve them.

I take this opportunity to write, by our committee who were sent to this colony, just to let you know that I am comfortable, and shall proceed this afternoon. Pray write to me, and get all my friends to write, and let me be informed of every thing that occurs. Send your letters to Colonel Palmer, or Doctor Warren, who will convey them. They will reach me sooner or later. This colony is raising six thousand men. Rhode Island, fifteen hundred. New York has shut up their port, seized the Custom House, arms, ammunition, &c., called a provincial Congress, and entered into an association to stand by whatever shall be ordered by the continental and their provincial Congress. Dr. Cooper is fled on board a man of war, and the tories are humbled in the dust.

Tell my brothers I have bought some military books, and intend to buy more, so that I shall come back qualified to make them complete officers. Write me whether either of them intends to take a command in the army. I won't advise them, but leave them to their own inclinations and discretion. But, if they should incline, they should apply to Colonel Palmer and Dr. Warren soon.

LETTER XIX.[1]

Hartford, 2 May, 1775.

MY DEAR,

MR. ELIOT, of Fairfield, is this moment arrived, on his way to Boston. He read us a letter from the Doctor, his father, dated yesterday sennight, being Sunday. The Doctor's description of the melancholy of the town, is enough to melt a stone. The trials of that unhappy and devoted people are likely to be severe indeed. God grant that the furnace of affliction may refine them. God grant that they may be relieved from their present distress.

It is arrogance and presumption, in human sagacity, to pretend to penetrate far into the designs of Heaven. The most perfect reverence and resignation becomes us, but I cannot help depending upon this, that the present dreadful calamity of that beloved town, is intended to bind the colonies together in more indissoluble bonds, and to animate their exertions at this great crisis in the affairs of mankind. It has this effect in a most remarkable degree, as far as I have yet seen or heard. It will plead with all America with more irresistible persuasion than angels trumpet-tongued.

In a cause which interests the whole globe, at a

---

[1] This letter appears to have been written after the preceding one had been sent, and in consequence of receiving intelligence of the affair at Lexington, of the 19th of April.

time when my friends and country are in such keen distress, I am scarcely ever interrupted in the least degree by apprehensions for my personal safety. I am often concerned for you and our dear babes, surrounded, as you are, by people who are too timorous, and too much susceptible of alarms. Many fears and jealousies and imaginary dangers will be suggested to you, but I hope you will not be impressed by them. In case of real danger, of which you cannot fail to have previous intimations, fly to the woods with our children. Give my tenderest love to them, and to all.

LETTER XX.

Philadelphia, 29 May, 1775.

MY DEAR,

Our amiable friend Hancock, who, by the way, is our President, is to send his servant tomorrow for Cambridge. I am to send a few lines by him. If his man should come to you, to deliver this letter, treat him very kindly, because he is a kind, humane, clever fellow.

We are distressed here for want of intelligence and information from you and from Boston, Cambridge, &c. &c. &c. We have no regular advices. I received one kind letter from you in one from Colonel Warren. An excellent letter I had from him. It has done him great honor and me much

good. My duty and love to all. I have had miserable health and blind eyes, almost ever since I left
you; but I found Dr. Young here, who, after scolding
at me quantum sufficit, for not taking his advice, has
pill'd and electuary'd me into pretty good order.
My eyes are better, my head is better, so are my
spirits.

The Congress will support the Massachusetts.
There is a good spirit here. But we have an amazing field of business before us. When I shall have
the joy of meeting you and our little ones, I know not.
The military spirit, which runs through the continent,
is truly amazing. This city turns out two thousand
men every day. Mr. Dickinson is a Colonel, Mr.
Reed a Lieutenant-Colonel, Mr. Mifflin. a Major.
He ought to have been a General, for he has been
the animating soul of the whole.

Colonel Washington appears at Congress, in his
uniform, and, by his great experience and abilities
in military matters, is of much service to us.

Oh that I were a soldier! I will be. I am reading
military books. Every body must, and will, and
shall be a soldier.

JOHN ADAMS.

LETTER XXI.

Philadelphia, 10 June, 1775.

MY DEAR,

DOCTOR CHURCH returns to-day, and, with smarting eyes, I must write a few lines to you. I never had in my life such severe duty to do, and was never worse qualified to do it. My eyes depress my spirits, and my health is quite infirm. Yet I keep about, and attend Congress very constantly.

I wish I could write freely to you, my dear, but I cannot. The scene before me is complicated enough. It requires better eyes, and better nerves than mine ; yet I will not despond. I will lay all difficulties prostrate at my feet. My health and life ought to be hazarded in the cause of my country, as well as your's, and all my friends.

It is impossible to convey, to you any adequate idea of the embarrassments I am under. I wish that you and our friends may not be in greater distress than I am. I fear you are. Pray let me know as often as possible. Our friends write to Mr. —, not to me, this time. They don't let us know the state of Boston people, nor the state of the army in Boston, so exactly as I could wish.

Two days ago we saw a very wonderful phenomenon in this city ; a field day, on which three battalions of soldiers were reviewed, making full two thousand men, battalion men, light infantry, grena-

diers, riflemen, light horse, artillery men with a fine
train, all in uniforms, going through the manual exercise, and the manœuvres, with remarkable dexterity.   All this has been accomplished in this city since
the 19th of April; so sudden a formation of an
army never took place any where.

In Congress we are bound to secrecy.   But, under
the rose, I believe that ten thousand men will be maintained in the Massachusetts, and five thousand in
New York, at the continental expense.

We have a major Skene, just arrived from London
with a commission to be Governor of Crown Point
and Ticonderoga, and surveyor of the woods, &c.,
a close prisoner.   He must dispute for his government
with Arnold and Allen.

My love and duty where due.

LETTER XXII.

Philadelphia, 10 June, 1775.

MY DEAR,

DR. CHURCH has given me a lotion which has helped
my eyes so much that I hope you will hear from me
oftener than you have done.   Pray write me as often
and particularly as possible.   Send your letters to the
care of the Committee of Safety, who will forward
them.   I long to know how you fare, and whether
you are often discomposed with alarms.   Guard your-

self against them, my dear. I think you are in no danger. Don't let the groundless fears and fruitful imaginations of others affect you. Let me know what guards are kept; and who were principally concerned in the battle[1] at Grape Island, as well as that at Chelsea. The reputation of our country-men for valor is very high. I hope they will main-tain it, as well as that for prudence, caution, and con-duct.

When I shall come home I know not. We have business enough before us, to detain us until the 31st of next December. No assembly ever had a greater number of great objects before them. Provinces, Nations, Empires are small things before us. I wish we were good architects.

LETTER XXIII.

Philadelphia, 11 June, 1775.

MY DEAR,

I HAVE been this morning to hear Mr. Duffield, a preach-er in this city, whose principles, prayers and sermons, more nearly resemble those of our New England clergy, than any that I have heard. His discourse was a kind of exposition on the thirty-fifth chapter of Isaiah. America was the wilderness, and the

---

[1] Mrs. Adams's letter of 24 May, Vol. I. p. 32.

solitary place, and he said it would be glad, "rejoice
and blossom as the rose." He laboured " to strengthen
the weak hands and confirm the feeble knees." He
"said to them that were of a fearful heart, Be strong,
fear not. Behold, your God will come with vengeance,
even God with a recompense ; he will come and save
you." " No lion shall be there, nor any ravenous beast
shall go up thereon, but the redeemed shall walk
there, &c." He applied the whole prophecy to this
country, and gave us as animating an entertainment
as I ever heard. He filled and swelled the bosom
of every hearer. I hope you have received a letter,
in which I inclosed you a pastoral letter from the
synod of New York and Philadelphia; by this you
will see, that the Clergy this way are but now beginning to engage in politics, and they engage with a
fervor that will produce wonderful effects.

17 June.

I can now inform you, that the Congress have made
choice of the modest and virtuous, the amiable, generous and brave George Washington, Esquire, to be
General of the American army, and that he is to re-
pair, as soon as possible, to the camp before Boston.
This appointment will have a great effect in cement-
ing and securing the union of these colonies. The
continent is really in earnest, in defending the country. They have voted ten companies of riflemen to
be sent from Pennsylvania, Maryland and Virginia,

to join the army before Boston. These are an excellent species of light infantry. They use a peculiar kind
of musket, called a rifle. It has circular or —[1] grooves
within the barrel, and carries a ball with great exact-
ness to great distances. They are the most accurate
marksmen in the world.

I begin to hope we shall not sit all summer. I
hope the people of our province will treat the General
with all that confidence and affection, that politeness
and respect, which is due to one of the most important characters in the world. The liberties of America depend upon him, in a great degree. I have never
been able to obtain from our province any regular and
particular intelligence, since I left it. Kent, Swift,
Tudor, Dr. Cooper, Dr. Winthrop and others wrote
me often last fall; not a line from them this time.

I have found this Congress like the last. When
we first came together, I found a strong jealousy of us
from New England, and the Massachusetts in particular. Suspicions entertained of designs of independency; an American republic; presbyterian principles, and twenty other things. Our sentiments were
heard in Congress with great caution, and seemed to
make but little impression; but the longer we sat,
the more clearly they saw the necessity of pushing
vigorous measures. It has been so now. Every day
we sit, the more we are convinced that the designs
against us are hostile and sanguinary, and that nothing but fortitude, vigor, and perseverance can save us.

But America is a great unwieldy body. Its pro-

---

[1] The manuscript is defective here.

gress must be slow. It is like a large fleet sailing under convoy. The fleetest sailers must wait for the dullest and slowest. Like a coach and six, the swiftest horses must be slackened, and the slowest quickened, that all may keep an even pace.

It is long since I heard from you. I fear you have been kept in continual alarms. My duty and love to all. My dear children, come here and kiss me. We have appointed a continental fast. Millions will be upon their knees at once before their great Creator, imploring his forgiveness and blessing; his smiles on American councils and arms.

My duty to your uncle Quincy; your papa, mamma, and mine; my brothers and sisters, and yours.

Adieu.

———

LETTER XXIV.

Philadelphia, 18 June, 1775.

MY DEAR,

THIS letter, I presume, will go by the brave and amiable General Washington. Our army will have a group of officers equal to any service. Washington, Ward, Lee, Gates, Gridley, together with all the other New England officers, will make a glorious council of war.

This Congress are all as deep as the delegates from the Massachusetts, and the whole continent as for-

ward as Boston. We shall have a redress of grievances, or an assumption of all the powers of Government, legislative, executive and judicial, throughout the whole Continent, very soon. Georgia is be-
stirring itself. I mean, the whole of it. The Parish
of St. John's, which is one third of it, was with us
before.

I am, &c.

LETTER XXV.

Philadelphia, 23 June, 1775.

MY DEAR,

I HAVE this morning been out of town, to accompany
our Generals, Washington, Lee and Schuyler, a little
way on their journey to the American camp, before
Boston. The three Generals were all mounted on
horse-back, accompanied by Major Mifflin, who is
gone in the character of Aid-de-camp. All the
delegates from the Massachusetts, with their servants
and carriages, attended. Many others of the delegates
from the Congress ; a large troop of light horse in
their uniforms ; many officers of militia, besides, in
their's; music playing, &c. &c. Such is the pride and
pomp of war. I, poor creature, worn out with scribbling for my bread and my liberty, low in spirits and
weak in health, must leave others to wear the laurels

which I have sown ; others to eat the bread which I have earned ; a common case.

We had, yesterday, by the way of New York and New London, a report which distresses us almost as much as that we had last fall, of the cannonade of Boston. A battle at Bunker's hill, and Dorchester point. Three Colonels wounded, *Gardner* mortally. We wait to hear more particulars. Our hopes and fears are, alternately, very strong. If there is any truth in this account, you must be in great confusion. God Almighty's providence preserve, sustain, and comfort you.

27 June.

This moment received two letters[1] from you. Courage, my dear. We shall be supported in life or comforted in death. I rejoice that my countrymen behaved so bravely, though not so skilfully conducted as I could wish. I hope this defect will be remedied by the new modelling of the army.

My love every where.

[1] Mrs. Adams's letters of 15 and 18 June, 1775. Vol. I. p. 35 and 39.

LETTER XXVI.

Philadelphia, 7 July, 1775.

MY DEAR,

I HAVE received your very agreeable favors [1] of June
22 and 25. They contain more particulars than any
letters I had before received from anybody.

It is not at all surprising to me, that the wanton,
cruel, and infamous conflagration of Charlestown, the
place of your father's nativity, should afflict him.
Let him know that I sincerely condole with him on that
melancholy event. It is a method of conducting war
long since become disreputable among civilized nations. But every year brings us fresh evidence that
we have nothing to hope for, from our loving mother
country, but cruelties more abominable than those
which are practised by the savage Indians.

The account you give me of the numbers slain on
the side of our enemies, is afflicting to humanity,
although it is a glorious proof of the bravery of our
worthy countrymen. Considering all the disadvantages under which they fought, they really exhibited
prodigies of valor. Your description of the distresses
of the worthy inhabitants of Boston and the other
seaport towns, is enough to melt a heart of stone.
Our consolation must be this, my dear, that cities

---

[1] These will be found among the letters of Mrs. Adams,
Vol. I. pp. 41 and 43.

may be rebuilt, and a people, reduced to poverty, may acquire fresh property. But a constitution of government, once changed from freedom, can never be restored. Liberty once lost, is lost forever. When the people once surrender their share in the Legislature, and their right of defending the limitations upon the Government, and of resisting every encroachment upon them, they can never regain it.

The loss of Mr. Mather's library, which was a collection of books and manuscripts made by himself, his father, his grandfather, and great-grandfather, and was really very curious and valuable, is irreparable. The family picture you draw is charming indeed. My dear Abby, Johnny, Charley and Tommy, I long to see you, and to share with your mamma the pleasures of your conversation. I feel myself much obliged to Mr. Bowdoin, Mr. Wibird and the two families you mention for their civilities to you. My compliments to them. Does Mr. Wibird preach against oppression and the other cardinal vices of the times ? Tell him, the clergy here of every denomination, not excepting the Episcopalian, thunder and lighten every Sabbath. They pray for Boston and the Massachusetts. They thank God most explicitly and fervently for our remarkable successes. They pray for the American army. They seem to feel as if they were among you.

You ask if every member feels for us ? Every member says he does, and most of them really do. But most of them feel more for themselves. In every society of men, in every club I ever yet saw, you find

some who are timid, their fears hurry them away upon every alarm. Some who are selfish and avaricious, on whose callous hearts nothing but interest
and money can make impression. There are some
persons in New York and Philadelphia, to whom a
ship is dearer than a city, and a few barrels of flour
than a thousand lives — other men's lives, I mean.

You ask, can they realize what we suffer? I
answer, no. They can't. They don't. And, to excuse them as well as I can, I must confess, I should
not be able to do it myself, if I was not more acquainted with it by experience than they are.

I am grieved for Dr. Tuft's ill health, but rejoiced exceedingly at his virtuous exertions in the cause of his
country. I am happy to hear that my brothers were
at Grape Island, and behaved well. My love to them,
and duty to my mother.

It gives me more pleasure than I can express, to
learn that you sustain with so much fortitude, the
shocks and terrors of the times. You are really
brave, my dear. You are a heroine, and you have
reason to be. For the worst that can happen, can do
you no harm. A soul as pure, as benevolent, as virtuous and pious as yours, has nothing to fear, but
everything to hope and expect from the last of human
evils. I am glad you have secured an asylum, though
I hope you will not have occasion for it.

There is an amiable, ingenious hussy, named Betsey
Smith, for whom I have a very great regard. Be pleased
to make my love acceptable to her, and let her know
that her elegant pen cannot be more usefully em-

ployed than in writing letters to her brother at Philadelphia, though it may be more agreeably, in writing
billets-doux to young gentlemen.

The other day, after I had received a letter of
yours, with one or two others, Mr. William Barrell
desired to read them. I put them into his hand, and
the next morning had them returned in a large bundle
packed up with two great heaps of pins, with a very polite card requesting Portia's acceptance of them.[1] I
shall bring them with me when I return. But when
that will be, is uncertain. I hope, not more than a
month hence.

I have really had a very disagreeable time of it.
My health, and especially my eyes, have been so very
bad, that I have not been so fit for business as I ought,
and if I had been in perfect health, I should have had,
in the present condition of my country and my friends,
no taste for pleasure. But Dr. Young has made a
kind of cure of my health, and Dr. Church of my
eyes.

I have received two kind letters from your uncle
Smith. Do thank him for them. I shall forever love
him for them. I love everybody that writes to me.

I am, forever yours.

---

[1] See the letters of Mrs. Adams, Vol. I. p. 39.

LETTER XXVII.

Philadelphia, 23 July, 1775.

MY DEAR,

You have more than once, in your letters,[1] mentioned Dr. Franklin, and in one, intimated a desire that I should write you something concerning him.

Dr. Franklin has been very constant in his attendance on Congress from the beginning. His conduct has been composed and grave, and, in the opinion of many gentlemen, very reserved. He has not assumed any thing, nor affected to take the lead; but has seemed to choose that the Congress should pursue their own principles and sentiments, and adopt their own plans. Yet he has not been backward; has been very useful on many occasions, and discovered a disposition entirely American. He does not hesitate at our boldest measures, but rather seems to think us too irresolute and backward. He thinks us at present in an odd state, neither in peace nor war, neither dependent nor independent; but he thinks that we shall soon assume a character more decisive. He thinks that we have the power of preserving ourselves; and that even if we should be driven to the disagreeable necessity of assuming a total independency, and set up a separate state, we can maintain it. The people of England have thought

[1] Letters of Mrs. Adams, Vol. I. pp. 34 and 49.

that the opposition in America, was wholly owing to
Dr. Franklin; and I suppose their scribblers will attribute the temper and proceedings of Congress to
him; but there cannot be a greater mistake. He
has had but little share, further than to coöperate
and to assist. He is however a great and good man.
I wish his colleagues from this city were all like him;
particularly one,[1] whose abilities and virtues, formerly
trumpeted so much in America, have been found
wanting. There is a young gentleman from Pennsylvania, whose name is Wilson, whose fortitude, rectitude and abilities too, greatly outshine his master's.
Mr. Biddle, the Speaker, has been taken off by sick-
ness, Mr. Mifflin is gone to the camp, Mr. Morton is
ill too, so that this province has suffered by the timidity of two overgrown fortunes. The dread of con-
fiscation or caprice, I know not what, has influenced
them too much; yet they were for taking arms, and
pretended to be very valiant.

This letter must be secret, my dear; at least, communicated with great discretion.

Yours,

JOHN ADAMS.

---

[1] An allusion to John Dickinson. He had labored hard and
successfully to procure the adoption, by Congress, of a second
petition to the King, against the opinion of many among the
more zealous patriots; and this gave rise to the idea that he
was lukewarm in the cause of resistance. See Gordon s History, Vol. I. p. 32.

LETTER XXVIII.

Philadelphia, 30 July, 1775.

MY DEAR.

THIS letter is intended to go by my friend Mr. William Barrell, whom I believe you have seen in Boston. If he calls at our house you will please to receive him complaisantly, and thank him for your present of pins. I have been treated by him with great civility, both at this, and the former Congress.

This day I have heard my parish priest, Mr. Duffield, from Chronicles xv. 1, 2. This gentleman never fails to adapt his discourse to the times. He pressed upon his audience the necessity of piety and virtue in the present times of adversity, and held up to their view the army before Boston, as an example. He understood, he said, that the voice of the swearer was scarcely heard ; that the Sabbath was well observed, and all immoralities discountenanced. No doubt there were vicious individuals, but the general character was good. I hope this good man's information is true, and that this will become more and more the true character of that camp. You may well suppose that this language was exceedingly pleasing to me.

We have nothing new, but the arrival of some powder. Three little vessels have certainly arrived, making about ten tons in the whole, and four or five tons have arrived from South Carolina. A supply, I think now we shall certainly obtain. Congress have taken measures for this end, which I hope to have the pleasure of explaining to you, in person, within a few days, as Congress have determined to adjourn to some time in September. I could not vote for this myself, because I thought it might be necessary to keep together ; but I could not blame those who did, for really we have been all so assiduous in business, in this exhausting, debilitating climate, that our lives are more exposed than they would be in camp.

Love to the children.

LETTER XXIX.

Philadelphia, 1 October, 1775.

MY DEAR,

THIS morning I received your two letters of 8 September and 16 September. What shall I say ? The intelligence they contain came upon me by surprise, as I never had the least intimation before, that any of my family was ill, excepting in a card from Mrs. Warren, received a few days ago, in which she informed me, that Mrs. Adams had been unwell, but was better.

You may easily conceive the state of mind in which I am at present. Uncertain and apprehensive, at first, I suddenly thought of setting off immediately for Braintree, and I have not yet determined otherwise. Yet the state of public affairs is so critical, that

I am half afraid to leave my station, although my presence here is of no great consequence.

I feel, I tremble for you. Poor Tommy! I hope, by this time, however, he has recovered his plump cheeks, and his fine bloom. By your account of Patty, I fear, but still I will hope she has been supported, and is upon the recovery. I rejoice to learn that Abby and her brothers have hitherto escaped, and pray God that his goodness may be still continued to them. Your description of the distressed state of the neighbourhood is affecting indeed. It is not uncommon for a train of calamities to come together. Fire, sword, pestilence, famine often keep company and visit a country in a flock.

At this distance I can do no good to you or your's. I pray God to support you. I hope our friends and neighbours are kind as usual. I feel for them in the general calamity. I am so far from thinking you melancholy, that I am charmed with that admirable fortitude, and that divine spirit of resignation, which appear in your letters. I cannot express the satisfaction it gives me, nor how much it contributes to support me.

You have alarmed me, however, by mentioning anxieties which you do not think it proper to mention to any one. I am wholly at a loss to conjecture what they can be. If they arise from the letters, be assured that you may banish them forever. These letters [1]

---

[1] Certain letters written by Mr. Adams to James Warren and to his wife, which were intercepted by the enemy. They will be found, together with some account of the effect they produced at this time, in the Appendix to this volume, A.

have reached Philadelphia, but have produced effects very different from those which were expected from the publication of them. These effects I will explain to you sometime or other. As to the versification of them, if there is wit or humor in it, laugh — if ill nature, sneer — if mere dulness, why you may even yawn or nod. I have no anger at it, nay even scarcely contempt. It is impotent.

As to politics, we have nothing to expect but the whole wrath and force of Great Britain. But your words are as true as an oracle, " God helps them who help themselves, and if we obtain the divine aid by our own virtue, fortitude and perseverance, we may be sure of relief." It may amuse you to hear a story. A few days ago, in company with Dr. Zubly, somebody said, there was nobody on our side but the Almighty. The Doctor,[1] who is a native of Switzerland, and speaks but broken English, quickly replied, " Dat is enough. Dat is enough ;" and, turning to me, says he, " It puts me in mind of a fellow who once said, The Catholics have on their side the Pope, and the King of France, and the King of Spain, and the King of Sardinia, and the King of Poland, and the Emperor of Germany, &c., &c., &c. But as to those poor

[1] The Reverend Dr. Zubly was one of the Delegates to the Congress from Georgia, which province did not appoint any until July, 1775. He however was among the few who stopped by the way side. So far from retaining the confidence here expressed in the American cause, he entered into secret correspondence with the British authorities in Georgia, and being discovered, he fled the country.

devils, the protestants, they have nothing on their side
but God Almighty."

——

LETTER XXX.

Philadelphia, 2 October, 1775.

EVERYTHING here is in as good a way as I could wish,
considering the temper and designs of Administration.
I assure you, the letters have had no such bad effects
as the Tories intended, and as some of our short-
sighted Whigs apprehended ; so far otherwise, that I
see and hear, every day, fresh proofs that everybody
is coming fast into every political sentiment contained in them. I assure you I could mention compliments passed upon them, and if a serious decision
could be had upon them, the public voice would be
found in their favor.

But I am distressed with cares of another kind.
Your two letters are never out of my thoughts. I
should have mounted my horse, this day, for Braintree,
if I had not hopes of hearing further from you in a
day or two. However, I will hope that your prospects are more agreeable than they were, and that the
children are all better, as well as the rest of the family, and the neighbours. If I should hear more disagreeable advices from you, I shall certainly come
home, for I cannot leave you in such affliction without

endeavouring to lessen it, unless there was an absolute
necessity of my staying here to do a duty to the public, which I think there is not.

I must beg to be excused, my dear, from hinting at
anything for the future, of public persons or things.
Secrecy is so much exacted.   But thus much I may
say, that I never saw so serious and determined a
spirit.   I must also beseech you to be cautious what
you write to me and by whom you send.   Letters
sent to the care of Colonel Warren will come safe.
My regards, with all proper distinctions, to my relations and yours, my friends and yours, my acquaintances and yours.

This will go by Major Bayard, a gentleman of the
Presbyterian persuasion in this city, of excellent character, to whom I am indebted for a great many civilities.

LETTER XXXI.

Philadelphia, 7 October, 1775.

MY DEAR,

YESTERDAY, by the post, I received yours of 25 September.   And it renewed a grief and anxiety, that
were, before, almost removed from my mind.   Two
days before, I had the pleasure of a very valuable
letter from Colonel Quincy, in which he kindly informed me, that you and our family were so much

better, that you and my dear Abby had made a visit
at his house ; and Mr. Williams, who brought the letter, acquainted me, that he had been to Braintree after
the date of it, that you was in good spirits, that
Tommy was so much better as to be playing abroad,
and that he hoped Patty was not in danger. You will
easily believe that this information gave me great
pleasure and fine spirits. It really relieved me from
a heavy load. But your last letter has revived my
concern. I will still hope, however, that your excellent mother will yet be spared for a blessing to her
family, and an example to the world. I build my
hopes of her recovery upon the advantage of a constitution which has hitherto sustained so many attacks,
and upon a long course of exact temperance, which,
I hope, has deprived the distemper of its most dangerous food and fuel. However, our lives are not in
our own power. It is our duty to submit. " The ways
of Heaven are dark and intricate," its designs are
often inscrutable, but are always wise and just and
good.

It was long before I had the least intimation of the
distress of the family, and I fear, that your not receiving so many letters from me as usual, may have
been one cause of infelicity to you. Really, my dear,
I have been more cautious than I used to be. It is
not easy to know whom to trust in these times ; and
if a letter, from any person in the situation I am in,
can be laid hold of, there are so many lies made and
told about it, so many false copies taken and dis-
persed, and so many false constructions put, that one
ought to be cautious.

The situation of things is so alarming, that it is our duty to prepare our minds and hearts for every event, even the worst. From my earliest entrance into life, I have been engaged in the public cause of America; and from first to last, I have had upon my mind a strong impression that things would be wrought up to their present crisis. I saw, from the beginning, that the controversy was of such a nature, that it never would be settled, and every day convinces me more and more. This has been the source of all the disquietude of my life. It has lain down and risen up with me these twelve years. The thought, that we might be driven to the sad necessity of breaking our connexion with Great Britain, exclusive of the carnage and destruction, which, it was easy to see, must attend the separation, always gave me a great deal of grief. And even now, I would cheerfully retire from public life forever, renounce all chance for profits or honors from the public, nay, I would cheerfully contribute my little property, to obtain peace and liberty. But all these must go, and my life too, before I can surrender the right of my country to a free Constitution. I dare not consent to it. I should be the most miserable of mortals ever after, whatever honors or emoluments might surround me.

LETTER XXXII.

[Philadelphia], 10 October, 1775.

I AM much concerned lest you should feel an addition to your anxieties, from your having so seldom heard from me. But I pray you to dismiss all concern about me. I am happier far, than I was before the adjournment. My health is better, and business and conversation are much more to my taste.

The surprising intelligence we have in private letters concerning the Director of the Hospital,[1] has made me more cautious of writing than ever. I must be excused from writing a syllable of anything of any moment. My letters have been and will be nothing but trifles. I don't choose to trust the post. I am afraid to trust private travellers. They may peep. Accidents may happen ; and I would avoid, if I could, even ridicule, but especially mischief.

Pray, bundle up every paper, not already hid, and conceal them in impenetrable darkness. Nobody knows what may occur.

My love to those who are dearest to us both. Send yours to the care of the gentleman whose care has hitherto been successful. Date them in time, but not place, and assume a new fictitious name.

[1] Dr. Church.

LETTER XXXIII.

[Philadelphia], 13 October, 1775.

I THIS day received yours of the 29th of September and the 1st of October. Amidst all your afflictions, I am rejoiced to find that you all along preserve so proper and so happy a temper; that you are sensible " the consolations of religion are the only sure comforters." It is the constitution under which we are born, that if we live long ourselves, we must bury our parents, and all our elder relations, and many of those who are younger. I have lost a parent, a child and a brother, and each of them left a lasting impression on my mind. But you and I have many more relations and very good friends to follow to the house appointed for all flesh, or else we must be followed by them. I bewail, more than I can express, the loss of your excellent mother. I mourn the loss of so much purity, and unaffected piety and virtue, to the world. I know of no better character left in it. I grieve for you, and your brother and sisters. I grieve for your father, whose age will need the succor of so excellent a companion. But I grieve for nobody more than my children. Her most amiable and discreet example, as well as her kind skill and care, I have ever relied upon in my own mind, for the education of these little swarms. Not that I have not a proper esteem for the capacity and disposition of the mother, but I know that the efforts of the grandmother are of great importance, when they second those of the parent. And I am sure that my children are the better for the forming hand of their grandmother. It gives me great joy to learn that ours are well. Let us be thankful for this, and many other blessings yet granted us. Pray, my dear, cherish in their minds the remembrance of their grandmamma, and remind them of her precepts and example. God Almighty grant to you and to every branch of the family, all the support that you want.

You and I, my dear, have reason, if ever mortals had, to be thoughtful ; to look forward beyond the transitory scene. Whatever is preparing for us, let us be prepared to receive. It is time for us to subdue our passions of every kind. The prospect before us is an ocean of uncertainties, in which no pleasing objects appear. We have few hopes, excepting that of preserving our honor and our consciences untainted, and a free Constitution to our country. Let me be sure of these, and, amidst all my weaknesses, I cannot be overcome. With these, I can be happy in extreme poverty, in humble insignificance, may I hope and believe, in death : Without them, I should be miserable with a crown upon my head, millions in my coffers and a gaping, idolizing multitude at my feet.

My heart is too full of grief for you and our friends, to whom I wish you to present my regards, to say anything of news or politics. Yet the affair of the Surgeon-General is so strange and important an event, that I cannot close this gloomy letter without adding a sigh for this imprudent, unfortunate man. I know not whether the evidence will support the word treachery, but what may we not expect after treachery to himself, his wife and children?

LETTER XXXIV.

[Philadelphia], 19 October, 1775.

IT is some time since I wrote you, and I have nothing now to write, but repetitions of respect and affection. I am anxious to hear from you. I hope the family is better; that your grief for the great loss we have all sustained is somewhat abated. I hope your father and sister Betsey are well, though they must be greatly afflicted. Give my love to Betsey, and let her know that I feel most intimately for her, as well as for myself and the rest. I consider the stroke must fall heavier upon her, as it was nearer to her. Her prosperity is near my heart. I wish her every blessing which she can possibly wish for herself.

Really it is very painful to be four hundred miles from one's family and friends, when we know they are in affliction. It seems as if it would be a joy to me to fly home, even to share with you your burdens and misfortunes. Surely, if I were with you, it would be my study to allay your griefs, to mitigate your pains, and to divert your melancholy thoughts. When I shall come home, I know not. We have so much to do, and it is so difficult to do it right, that we must learn patience. Upon my word, I think, if ever I were to come here again, I must bring you with me. I could live here pleasantly, if I had you with me. Will you come and have the small pox[1] here? I wish I could remove all the family, our little daughter and sons, and all go through the distemper here. What if we should? Let me please myself with the thought however.

Congress has appointed Mr. Wythe, Mr. Deane and me, a Committee to collect an account of the hostilities committed by the troops and ships, with proper evidence of the number and value of the houses and other buildings destroyed or damaged, the vessels captivated, and the cattle, sheep, hogs, &c., taken. We are about writing to all the general assemblies of New England, and to many private gentlemen in each colony, to assist us in making the collections. The gentlemen with me are able men. Deane's character, you know. He is a very ingenious man and an able politician. Wythe is a new member from Virginia, a lawyer of the highest eminence in that province, a learned and very laborious man ; so that we may hope this commission will be well executed. A tale of woe it will be ! Such a scene of distress and destruction, and so patiently and magnanimously borne ! Such a scene of cruelty and barbarity, so unfeelingly committed ! I mention this to you, my

---

[1] By inoculation, as was then the practice.

dear, that you may look up, and transmit to me, a paper which Colonel Palmer lent me, containing a relation of the Charlestown battle, which was transmitted to England by the Committee of safety. This paper I must have, or a copy of it.

I wish I could collect, from the people of Boston or others, a proper set of paintings of the scenes of distress and misery brought upon that town from the commencement of the Port bill. Posterity must hear a story that shall make their ears to tingle.

Yours, yours, yours.

LETTER XXXV.

[Philadelphia], 23 October, 1775.

YESTERDAY, yours of October 9th came to hand. Your letters never failed to give me pleasure. The greatest pleasure that I take, is in receiving them. And although every one, which has yet come to hand, is replete with melancholy tidings, yet I can truly say, I never was so earnest to receive them. I rejoice in the happy principles and the happy temper which apparently dictated them all.

I feel myself much affected with the breach upon the family. But we can count a mother, a brother, an aunt, and a brother's child among the slain by this cruel pestilence. May God Almighty put a stop to its rage and humble us under the ravages already made by it. The sorrows of all our friends, on the loss of your mother, are never out of my mind. I pray God to spare my parent, whose life has been prolonged by his goodness hitherto, as well as yours that survives. The tremendous calamities already felt of fire, sword and pestilence may be only harbingers of greater still. We have no security against calamity here. This planet is its region. The only principle is to be prepared for the worst events.

If I could write as well as you, my sorrow would be as eloquent as yours, but, upon my word, I cannot.

The unaccountable event, which you allude to, has reached this place and occasioned a fall. I would be glad, however, that the worst construction might not be put. Let him [1] have fair play; though I doubt.

The man who violates private faith, cancels solemn obligations, whom neither honor nor conscience holds, shall never be knowingly trusted by me. Had I known, when I first voted for a Director of an Hospital, what I heard afterwards, when I was down, I would not have voted as I did. Open, barefaced immorality ought not to be so countenanced. Though I think a fatality attends us in some instances, yet a divine protection and favor is visible in others; and let us be cheerful, whatever happens. Cheerfulness is not a sin in any times.

I am afraid to hear again almost, lest some other should be sick in the house. Yet I hope better, and

Dr. Church.

that you will reassume your wonted cheerfulness and write again upon news and politics. Send your letters to Warren for conveyance. I won't trust any other.

LETTER XXXVI.

[Philadelphia[1]], 29 October, 1775.

I CANNOT exclude from my mind your melancholy situation. The griefs of your father and sisters, your uncles and aunts, as well as the remoter connexions, often crowd in upon me, when my whole attention ought to be directed to other subjects. Your uncle Quincy, my friend as well as uncle, must regret the loss of a beloved sister. Doctor Tufts, my other friend, I know, bewails the loss of a friend, as well as an aunt and a sister. Mr. Cranch, the friend of my youth, as well as of my riper years, whose tender heart sympathizes with his fellow creatures in every affliction and distress, in this case, feels the loss of a friend, a fellow christian and a mother. But, alas! what avail these mournful reflections? The best thing we can do, the greatest respect we can show to the

---

[1] Wherever the name of the place, from which a letter was dated, appears within brackets, it has been supplied, for the convenience of the reader. It was originally suppressed, together with the signature, for the reason given in p. 63, at the bottom.

memory of our departed friend, is to copy into our
own lives, those virtues which, in her lifetime, rendered her the object of our esteem, love and admiration.   I must confess, I ever felt a veneration for her,
which seems increased by the news of her transla-
tion.

Above all things, my dear, let us inculcate these
great virtues and bright excellencies upon our children.

Your mother had a clear and penetrating understanding, and a profound judgment, as well as an
honest, and a friendly and a charitable heart. There is
one thing, however, which you will forgive me if I
hint to you.   Let me ask you rather, if you are not
of my opinion ?   Were not her talents and virtues
too much confined to private, social and domestic life ?
My opinion of the duties of religion and morality
comprehends a very extensive connexion with society
at large and the great interests of the public.   Does
not natural morality and much more christian benevolence make it our indispensable duty to lay ourselves
out to serve our fellow creatures, to the utmost of our
power, in promoting and supporting those great political systems and general regulations, upon which the
happiness of multitudes depends ?   The benevolence,
charity, capacity and industry which, exerted in private life, would make a family, a parish or a town
happy, employed upon a larger scale, in support of
the great principles of virtue and freedom of political
regulations, might secure whole nations and generations from misery, want and contempt.   Public vir-

tues and political qualities therefore should be inces-
santly cherished in our children.

LETTER XXXVII.

[Philadelphia], 29 October, 1775.

HUMAN nature with all its infirmities and depravation
is still capable of great things. It is capable of attaining to degrees of wisdom and of goodness, which,
we have reason to believe, appear respectable in the
estimation of superior intelligences. Education makes
a greater difference between man and man, than nature has made between man and brute. The virtues
and powers to which men may be trained, by early
education and constant discipline, are truly sublime
and astonishing. Newton and Locke are examples
of the deep sagacity which may be acquired by long
habits of thinking and study. Nay, your common me-
chanics and artisans are proofs of the wonderful dexterity acquired by use; a watchmaker, in finishing
his wheels and springs, a pin or needlemaker, &c. I
think there is a particular occupation in Europe,
which is called a paper-stainer or linen-stainer. A
man who has been long habituated to it, shall sit for
a whole day, and draw upon paper fresh figures to be
imprinted upon the papers for rooms, as fast as his
eye can roll, and his fingers move, and no two of his

draughts shall be alike. The Saracens, the Knights of Malta, the army and navy in the service of the English republic, among many others, are instances to show, to what an exalted height valor or bravery or courage may be raised, by artificial means.

It should be your care, therefore, and mine, to elevate the minds of our children and exalt their courage; to accelerate and animate their industry and activity; to excite in them an habitual contempt of meanness, abhorrence of injustice and inhumanity, and an ambition to excel in every capacity, faculty and virtue. If we suffer their minds to grovel and creep in infancy, they will grovel all their lives.

But their bodies must be hardened, as well as their souls exalted. Without strength and activity and vigor of body, the brightest mental excellencies will be eclipsed and obscured.

LETTER XXXVIII.

[Philadelphia], 29 October, 1775.

THERE is in the human breast, a social affection, which extends to our whole species, faintly indeed, but in some degree. The nation, kingdom or community to which we belong is embraced by it more vigorously. It is stronger still towards the province to which we belong, and in which we had our birth. It is stronger and stronger as we descend to the county, town, parish, neighbourhood and family, which we call our own.   And here we find it often so powerful, as to become partial, to blind our eyes, to darken our understandings, and pervert our wills.

It is to this infirmity in my own heart, that I must perhaps attribute that local attachment, that partial fondness, that overweening prejudice in favor of New England, which I feel very often, and which, I fear, sometimes leads me to expose myself to just ridicule.

New England has, in many respects, the advantage of every other colony in America, and, indeed, of every other part of the world that I know any thing of.

1. The people are purer English blood ; less mixed with Scotch, Irish, Dutch, French, Danish, Swedish, &c., than any other; and descended from Englishmen too, who left Europe in purer times than the present, and less tainted with corruption than those they left behind them.

2. The institutions in New England for the support of religion, morals and decency exceed any other ; obliging every parish to have a minister, and every person to go to meeting, &c.

3. The public institutions in New England for the education of youth, supporting colleges at the public expense, and obliging towns to maintain grammar schools, are not equalled, and never were, in any part of the world.

4. The division of our territory, that is, our counties, into townships ; empowering towns to assemble,

choose officers, make laws, mend roads and twenty other things, gives every man an opportunity of showing and improving that education, which he received at college or at school, and makes knowledge and dexterity at public business common.

5. Our law for the distribution of intestate estates occasions a frequent division of landed property and prevents monopolies of land.

But in opposition to these we have labored under many disadvantages. The exorbitant prerogative of our Governors, &c., which would have overborne our liberties, if it had not been opposed by the five preceding particulars.

LETTER XXXIX.

[Philadelphia], 4 November, 1775.

I HAVE but yesterday received yours of October 21. Your letters of the following dates I have received, 8 and 10, 16, 29 September ; 1, 9, 21 and 22 October.[1] These letters, and indeed every line from you, give me inexpressible pleasure, notwithstanding the melancholy scenes described in most of them of late. I am happy to learn that the family is in health once

---

[1] See the letters of Mrs. Adams, Vol. I. pp. 67, *et seq.* for three of these letters. Extracts only from the rest were given in the Memoir, for reasons there stated, pp. xlii. *et seq.*

more, and hope it will continue. My duty to my
mother. I wish she would not be concerned about
me. She ought to consider, that a dysentery can kill
as surely as a cannon. This town is as secure from
the cannon and men of war as the moon is. I wish
she had a little of your fortitude. I had rather be
killed by a ball than live in such continual fears as
she does.

I can't write as often as I wish. I am engaged
from seven in the morning till eleven at night.

Two pair of colors, belonging to the seventh regiment, were brought here last night from Chambly, and
hung up in Mrs. Hancock's chamber with great splendor and elegance. That lady sends her compliments
and good wishes. Among a hundred men, almost, at
this house, she lives and behaves with modesty, decency, dignity and discretion, I assure you. Her
behaviour is easy and genteel. She avoids talking
upon politics. In large and mixed companies she is
totally silent, as a lady ought to be ; but whether her
eyes are so penetrating, and her attention so quick to
the words, looks, gestures, sentiments, &c., of the
company, as yours would be, saucy as you are this
way, I won't say.

But to resume a more serious subject. You ask me
to write to your father and sister, and my heart wishes
and longs to do it, but you can have no conception
what there is to prevent me. I really fear I shall
ruin myself for want of exercise.

LETTER XL.

[Philadelphia], 3 December, 1775.

MY BEST FRIEND,

YOURS of November 12th[1] is before me. I wish I could write you every day, more than once, for although I have a number of friends and many relations, who are very dear to me, yet all the friendship I have for others is far unequal to that which warms my heart for you. The most agreeable time that I spend here is in writing to you, and conversing with you, when I am alone. But the call of friendship and of private affection must give place to that of duty and honor. Even private friendship and affections require it.

I am obliged, by the nature of the service I am in, to correspond with many gentlemen, both of the army and of the two houses of Assembly, which takes up much of my time. How I find time to write half the letters I do, I know not, for my whole time seems engrossed with business. The whole Congress is taken up, almost, in different committees, from seven to ten in the morning. From ten to four or sometimes five, we are in Congress, and from six to ten, in committees again. I don't mention this to make you think me a man of importance, because it is not I alone,[2] but the

---

[1] Letters of Mrs. Adams, Vol. I. p. 78.

[2] During Mr. Adams's term of service in Congress, "he was a member of ninety, and chairman of twenty-five committees.

whole Congress is thus employed, but to apologize for not writing to you oftener.

Indeed I know not what to write that is worth your reading. I send you the papers, which inform you of what is public. As to what passes in Congress, I am tied fast by my honor to communicate nothing. I hope the Journal of the Session will be published soon, and then you will see what we have been about in one view, excepting what ought to be excepted. If I could visit the coffee-houses in the evening, and the coffee-tables of the ladies in the afternoon, I could entertain you with many smart remarks upon dress and air, &c., and give you many sprightly conversations, but my fate, you know, is to be moping over books and papers all the leisure time I have, when I have any.

I hope I shall be excused from coming to Philadelphia again, at least until other gentlemen have taken their turns. But I never will come here again without you, if I can persuade you to come with me. Whom God has joined together ought not to be put asunder so long, with their own consent. We will bring master Johnny with us; you and he shall have the small pox here, and we will be as happy as Mr. Hancock and his lady. Thank Abby and John for their letters and kiss Charles and Tom for me. John writes like a

A greater number than any other delegate, and twice as many as any but Samuel Adams and Richard Henry Lee." Biography of the Signers to the Declaration of Independence, Article, John Adams, Vol. viii. p. 280.

hero, glowing with ardor for his country and burning with indignation against her enemies.

As to coming home I have no thoughts of it ; shall stay here till the year is out, for what I know. Affairs are in a critical state, and important steps are now taking every day, so that I could not reconcile it to my own mind to be absent from this place at present. Nothing is expected from the Commissioners, yet we are waiting for them in some respects. The tories and timids pretend to expect great things from them. But the generality expect nothing but more insults and affronts. Privateering is licensed, and the ports are wide open. As soon as the resolves are printed, which will be to-morrow, I will send them.

LETTER XLI.

Watertown, 24 January, 1776.

MY DEAR,

I AM determined not to commit a fault, which escaped me the last time I set out for the southward. I waited on General Thomas at Roxbury, this morning, and then went to Cambridge, where I dined at Colonel Mifflin's with the General and lady, and a vast collec-

¹ This was upon Mr. Adams's departure from home to join the Congress for the third time.

tion of other company, among whom were six or seven sachems and warriors of the French Caghnawaga Indians with several of their wives and children. A savage feast they made of it, yet were very polite in the Indian style. One of these sachems is an English-man, a native of this colony, whose name was Wil-liams, captivated in infancy with his mother, and adopted by some kind squaw; another, I think, is half French blood.

I was introduced to them by the General, as one of the grand council fire at Philadelphia, which made them prick up their ears. They came and shook hands with me, and made me low bows and scrapes, &c. In short, I was much pleased with this day's entertainment.

The General is to make them presents in clothes and trinkets. They have visited the lines at Cam-bridge, and are going to see those at Roxbury.

To-morrow we mount for the grand council fire, where I shall think often of my little brood at the foot of Penn's hill. Remember me particularly to each of the children. Tell them I charge them to be good, honest, active and industrious, for their own sakes as well as ours.

LETTER XLII.

Philadelphia, 11 February, 1776.

MY DEAR,

HERE I am again. Arrived last Thursday, in good health, although I had a cold journey. The weather, a great part of the way, was very severe, which prevented our making very quick progress. My companion was agreeable and made the journey much less tedious than it would have been.

I can form no judgment of the state of public opinions and principles here, as yet, nor any conjectures of what an hour may bring forth.

Have been to meeting, and heard Mr. Duffield from Jeremiah ii. 17. " Hast thou not procured this unto thyself, in that thou hast forsaken the Lord thy God, when he led thee by the way ? " He prayed very earnestly for Boston and New York, supposing the latter to be in danger of destruction. I, however, am not convinced that Vandeput will fire upon that town. It has too much Tory property to be destroyed by Tories. I hope it will be fortified and saved. If not, the question may be asked, " hast thou not procured this, &c ? "

To-morrow Doctor Smith is to deliver an oration in honor of the brave Montgomery. I will send it, as soon as it is out, to you. There is a deep anxiety, a kind of thoughtful melancholy, and in some, a lowness of spirits approaching to despondency, prevailing

through the southern colonies, at present, very similar
to what I have often observed in Boston, particularly
on the first news of the port bill, and last year about
this time, or a little later, when the bad news arrived
which dashed their fond hopes, with which they had
deluded themselves through the winter.   In this or a
similar condition we shall remain, I think, until late in
the spring, when some critical event will take place,
perhaps sooner.   But the arbiter of events, the sovereign of the world only knows, which way the torrent
will be turned.   Judging by experience, by probabili-
ties and by all appearances, I conclude, it will roll on
to dominion and glory, though the circumstances and
consequences may be bloody.

In such great changes and commotions, individuals
are but atoms.   It is scarcely worth while to consider
what the consequences will be to us.   What will be
the effects upon present and future millions, and millions of millions, is a question very interesting to benevolence, natural and christian.   God grant they
may, and I firmly believe they will, be happy.

LETTER XLIII.

[Philadelphia], February, 1776.

LEE is at York, and we have requested a battalion of
Philadelphia associators, together with a regiment of
Jersey minute men, to march to his assistance.   Lord

Sterling was there before with his regiment, so that there will be about a thousand men with Lee from Connecticut, about six hundred with Lord Sterling from the Jerseys, one battalion of about seven hundred and twenty minute men from Jersey, and one of the same number from Philadelphia. We shall soon have four battalions more, raised in Pennsylvania, to march to the same place, and one more in the Jerseys. Mr. Dickinson being the first Colonel and Commander of the first battalion too, claimed it as his right to march upon this occasion. Mr. Reed, formerly General Washington's Secretary, goes his lieutenant colonel. Mr. Dickinson's alacrity and spirit upon this occasion, which certainly becomes his character, and sets a fine example, is much talked of and applauded. This afternoon, the four battalions of the militia were together, and Mr. Dickinson mounted the rostrum to harangue them, which he did with great vehemence and pathos, as it is reported.

I suppose, if I could have made interest enough to have been chosen more than a lieutenant, I should march too, upon some such emergency; and possibly a contingency may happen, when it will be proper for me to do it still, in rank and file. I will not fail to march, if it should. In the beginning of a war, in colonies like this and Virginia, where the martial spirit is but just awakened, and the people are unaccustomed to arms, it may be proper and necessary for such popular orators as Henry and Dickinson to assume a military character. But I really think them both better statesmen than soldiers, though I cannot say they are not very good in the latter character. Henry's principles and systems are much more conformable to mine than the other's, however.

I feel, upon some of these occasions, a flow of spirits and an effort of imagination, very like an ambition to be engaged in the more active, gay, and dangerous scenes ; (dangerous, I say, but recall that word, for there is no course more dangerous than that which I am in.)   I have felt such passions all my lifetime, particularly in the year **1757,** when I longed more ardently to be a soldier, than I ever did to be a lawyer.   But I am too old, and too much worn with fatigues of study in my youth, and there is too little need, in my Province, of such assistance, for me to assume a uniform —

> " Non tali auxilio, nec defensoribus istis
>   Tempus eget."

I believe I must write you soon Lord Sterling's character, because I was vastly pleased with him. For the future I shall draw no characters but such as I like.   Pimps destroy all freedom of correspondence.

LETTER XLIV.

Philadelphia, 18 February, 1776.

MY DEAREST FRIEND,

I SENT you from New York a pamphlet intituled " Common Sense," written in vindication of doctrines,

which there is reason to expect, that the further en-
croachments of tyranny and depredations of oppression
will soon make the common faith; unless the cunning
ministry, by proposing negotiations and terms of reconciliation, should divert the present current from its
channel.

Reconciliation if practicable, and peace if attainable,
you very well know, would be as agreeable to my inclinations, and as advantageous to my interest, as to
any man's. But I see no prospect, no probability, no
possibility. And I cannot but despise the understanding, which sincerely expects an honorable peace, for
its credulity, and detest the hypocritical heart, which
pretends to expect it, when in truth it does not. The
newspapers here are full of free speculations, the
tendency of which you will easily discover. The
writers reason from topics which have been long in
contemplation and fully understood by the people at
large in New England, but have been attended to in
the southern colonies only by gentlemen of free spirits
and liberal minds, who are very few. I shall endeavour to enclose to you as many of the papers and
pamphlets as I can, as long as I stay here. Some
will go by this conveyance.

Dr. Franklin, Mr. Chase, and Mr. Charles Carroll of
Carrollton in Maryland, are chosen a committee to go
into Canada. The characters of the two first you
know. The last is not a member of Congress, but a
gentleman of independent fortune, perhaps the largest
in America, a hundred and fifty or two hundred thousand pounds sterling; educated in some university in

France, though a native of America, of great abilities
and learning, complete master of the French language, and a professor of the Roman Catholic religion, yet a warm, a firm, a zealous supporter of the
rights of America, in whose cause he has hazarded
his all. Mr. John Carroll, of Maryland, a Roman
Catholic priest and a Jesuit, is to go with the committee ; the priests in Canada having refused baptism and
absolution to our friends there. General Lee is to
command in that country, whose address, experience
and abilities, added to his fluency in the French language, will give him great advantages.

The events of war are uncertain. We cannot en-
sure success, but we can deserve it. I am happy in
this provision for that important department, because
I think it the best that could be made in our circumstances. Your prudence will direct you to communicate the circumstances of the priest, the jesuit, and the
Romish religion, only to such persons as can judge of
the measure upon large and generous principles, and
will not indiscreetly divulge it. The step was necessary, for the anathemas of the church are very terrible to our friends in Canada.

I wish I understood French as well as you. I
would have gone to Canada, if I had. I feel the want
of education every day, particularly of that language.
I pray, my dear, that you would not suffer your sons
or your daughter ever to feel a similar pain. It is in
your power to teach them French, and I, every day,
see more and more, that it will become a necessary
accomplishment of an American gentleman or lady.

Pray write me in your next the name of the author of your thin French grammar, which gives you the pronunciation of the French words in English letters, that is, which shows you how the same sounds would be signified by English vowels and consonants.

Write me as often as you can. Tell me all the news. Desire the children to write to me, and believe me to be theirs and yours.

———

LETTER XLV.

Philadelphia, 17 March, 1776.

MY DEAREST FRIEND,

OUR worthy friend, Frank Dana, arrived here last evening from New York, to which place he came lately from England in the packet. In company with him is a gentleman by the name of Wrixon, who has been a field officer in the British army, served all the last war in Germany, and has seen service in every part of Europe. He left the army some time ago, and studied law in the temple, in which science he made a great proficiency. He wrote, lately, a pamphlet under the title of " the Rights of Britons," which he has brought over with him. He is a friend of liberty, and thinks justly of the American question. He has great abilities, as well as experience in the military science, and is an able engineer. I hope we shall employ him.

The Baron de Woedtke we have made a Brigadier General, and ordered him to Canada. The testimonials in his favor I shall enclose to you. Mr. Dana's account, with which Mr. Wrixon's agrees, ought to extinguish, in every mind, all hopes of reconciliation with Great Britain. This delusive hope has done us great injuries, and if ever we are ruined, will be the cause of our fall. A hankering after the leeks of Egypt makes us forget the cruelty of her task masters.

I shall suffer many severe pains on your account for some days. By a vessel from Salem a cannonade was heard from dark till nine o'clock, last night was a week ago. Your vicinity to such scenes of carnage and desolation as, I fear, are now to be seen in Boston and its environs, will throw you into much distress, but I believe in my conscience, I feel more here than you do. The sound of cannon was not so terrible, when I was at Braintree, as it is here, though I hear it at four hundred miles distance.

You can't imagine what a mortification I sustain in not having received a single line from you since we parted. I suspect some villany in conveyance. By the relation of Mr. Dana, Mr. Wrixon and Mr. Temple, Mr. Hutchinson, Mr. Sewall and their associates are in great disgrace in England. Persons are ashamed to be seen to speak to them. They look despised and sunk.

I shall enclose an extract of a letter from Mons. Dubourg in Paris, and a testimonial in favor of our Prussian General.

Adieu.

LETTER XLVI.

[Philadelphia], 19 March, 1776.

YESTERDAY I had the long expected and much wished pleasure of a letter from you, of various dates from the 2d to the 10th March.[1] This is the first line I have received since I left you. I wrote you from Watertown, I believe, relating my feast at the Quarter Master General's with the Caghnawaga Indians, and from Framingham, an account of the ordnance there, and from New York I sent you a pamphlet. Hope you received these. Since I arrived here, I have written to you as often as I could.

I am much pleased with your caution in your letter, in avoiding names both of persons and places, or any other circumstances, which might designate to strangers the writer, or the person written to, or the persons mentioned. Characters and description will do as well.

The lie which, you say, occasioned such disputes at the tavern, was curious enough. Who could make and spread it ? I am much obliged to an uncle for his friendship. My worthy fellow citizens may be easy about me. I never can forsake what I take to be their interests. My own have never been considered by me in competition with theirs. My ease, my

---

[1] Letters of Mrs. Adams, Vol. I. p. 88.

domestic happiness, my rural pleasures, my little property, my personal liberty, my reputation, my life have
little weight and ever had in my own estimation, in
comparison of the great object of my country.
I can say of it with sincerity, as Horace says of virtue.
" To America only and her friends a friend."

You ask what is thought of " Common Sense."
Sensible men think there are some whims, some
sophisms, some artful addresses to superstitious notions,
some keen attempts upon the passions, in this pamphlet. But all agree there is a great deal of good
sense delivered in clear, simple, concise and nervous
style. His sentiments of the abilities of Amer'ca, and
of the difficulty of a reconciliation with Great Britain,
are generally approved. But his notions and plans of
continental government are not much applauded. Indeed this writer[1] has a better hand in pulling down
than building. It has been very generally propagated
through the continent that I wrote this pamphlet.
But although I could not have written anything in so
manly and striking a style, I flatter myself I should
have made a more respectable figure as an architect,
if I had undertaken such a work. This writer seems
to have very inadequate ideas of what is proper and
necessary to be done, in order to form constitutions
for single colonies, as well as a great model of union
for the whole.

Your distresses, which you have painted in such
lively colors, I feel in every line as I read. I dare

---

[1] Paine's subsequent career did not belie this early prognos-
tication.

not write all that I think upon this occasion. I wish
our people had taken possession of Nook's hill at the
same time when they got the other heights, and before
the militia was dismissed.

Poor cousin! I pity him. How much soever he
may lament certain letters,[1] I don't lament. I never
repent of what was no sin. Misfortunes may be borne
without whining. But if I can believe Mr. Dana, those
letters were much admired in England. I can't help
laughing when I write it, because they were really
such hasty crude scraps. If I could have foreseen
their fate, they should have been fit to be seen, and
worth all the noise they have made. Mr. Dana says
they were considered in England as containing a com-
prehensive idea of what was necessary to be done,
and as showing resolution enough to do it. Wretched
stuff as they really were, according to him they have
contributed somewhat towards making certain persons
to be thought the greatest statesmen in the world. So
much for vanity.

My love, duty, respects and compliments wherever
they belong. Virginia will be well defended. So
will New York. So will South Carolina. America
will, ere long, raise her voice aloud and assume a
bolder air.

[1] The intercepted letters already alluded to, some account
of which will be found in the Appendix to this volume. See
Mrs. Adams's letters, Vol. I. p. 93.

LETTER XLVII.

[Philadelphia], 29 March, 1776

I GIVE you joy of Boston and Charlestown, once more the habitation of Americans. I am waiting with great impatience for letters from you, which I know, will contain many particulars. We are taking precautions to defend every place that is in danger, the Carolinas, Virginia, New York, Canada. I can think of nothing but fortifying Boston harbor. I want more cannon than are to be had. I want a fortification upon Point Alderton, one upon Lovell's Island, one upon George's Island, several upon Long Island, one upon the Moon, one upon Squantum. I want to hear of half a dozen fire ships, and two or three hundred fire rafts prepared. I want to hear of row-galleys, floating batteries built, and booms laid across the channel in the narrows, and *Vaisseaux de Frise* sunk in it. I wish to hear that you are translating Braintree commons into the channel. No efforts, no expense are too extravagant for me to wish for, to fortify that harbor so as to make it impregnable. I hope every body will join and work until it is done.

We have this week lost a very valuable friend of the colonies in Governor Ward, of Rhode Island, by the small pox in the natural way. He never would hearken to his friends, who have been constantly advising him to be inoculated, ever since the first Congress began. But he would not be persuaded. Numbers, who have been inoculated, have gone through this distemper without any danger, or even confinement, but nothing would do. He must take it in the natural way, and die. He was an amiable and a sensible man, a steadfast friend to his country upon very pure principles. His funeral was attended with the same solemnities as Mr. Randolph's. Mr. Stillman being the Anabaptist minister here, of which persuasion was the Governor, was desired by Congress to preach a sermon, which he did with great applause.

Remember me as you ought.

LETTER XLVIII.

12 April, 1776.

I ENCLOSE a few sheets of paper[1] and will send more as fast as opportunities present.

Chesterfield's letters[2] are a chequered set. You would not choose to have them in your library. They are like Congreve's plays, stained with libertine morals and base principles.

[1] Such was the scarcity of writing paper, owing to the interruption of all business in Boston, that for a short period, Mr. Adams appears to have sent it from Philadelphia.

[2] Mrs. Adams had expressed, in one of her letters, a wish to read this book.

You will see by the papers the news, the specula-
tions, and the political plans of the day. The ports
are opened wide enough at last, and privateers are
allowed to prey upon British trade. This is not
independency, you know. What is? Why, government in every colony, a confederation among them
all, and treaties with foreign nations to acknowledge
us a sovereign state and all that. When these things
will be done, or any of them, time must discover.
Perhaps the time is near, perhaps a great way off.

LETTER XLIX.

[Philadelphia], 14 April, 1776.

You justly complain of my short letters, but the critical state of things and the multiplicity of avocations
must plead my excuse. You ask where the fleet is?
The enclosed papers will inform you. You ask, what
sort of defence Virginia can make?[1] I believe they
will make an able defence. Their militia and minute
men have been some time employed in training themselves, and they have nine battalions of regulars, as
they call them, maintained among them, under good
officers, at the continental expense. They have set up a
number of manufactories of fire-arms, which are

---

[1] Mrs. Adams's Letters, Vol. I. p. 93.

busily employed. They are tolerably supplied with powder, and are successful and assiduous in making saltpetre. Their neighbouring sister, or rather daughter colony of North Carolina, which is a warlike colony, and has several battalions at the continental expense, as well as a pretty good militia, are ready to assist them, and they are in very good spirits and seem determined to make a brave resistance. The gentry are very rich, and the common people very poor. This inequality of property gives an aristocratical turn to all their proceedings, and occasions a strong aversion in their patricians, to Common Sense.[1] But the spirit of these Barons is coming down and it must submit. It is very true, as you observe, they have been duped by Dunmore. But this is a common case. All the colonies are duped, more or less, at one time and another. A more egregious bubble was never blown up, than the story of Commissioners coming to treat with the Congress, yet it has gained credit like a charm, not only with, but against, the clearest evidence. I never shall forget the delusion which seized our best and most sagacious friends, the dear inhabitants of Boston, the winter before last. Credulity and the want of foresight are imperfections in the human character, that no politician can sufficiently guard against.

You give me some pleasure by your account of a certain house in Queen street. I had burned it long ago in imagination. It rises now to my view like a

[1] Possibly alluding to Paine's pamphlet, bearing that title. See the " Writings of Washington," Vol. iii. p. 347.

phœnix.　What shall I say of the Solicitor General ?
I pity his pretty children.　I pity his father and his
sisters.　I wish I could be clear that it is no moral
evil to pity him and his lady.　Upon repentance, they
will certainly have a large share in the compassions of
many.　But let us take warning, and give it to our
children.　Whenever vanity and gaiety, a love of
pomp and dress, furniture, equipage, buildings, great
company, expensive diversions and elegant entertain-
ments get the better of the principles and judgments
of men or women, there is no knowing where they
will stop, nor into what evils, natural, moral or political they will lead us.　Your description of your own
gaieté de cœur charms me.　Thanks be to God, you
have just cause to rejoice ; and may the bright prospect be obscured by no cloud.　As to declarations of
independency, be patient.　Read our privateering
laws and our commercial laws.　What signifies a
word ?

As to your extraordinary code of laws, I cannot but
laugh.　We have been told that our struggle has loos-
ened the bonds of government every where ; that
children and apprentices were disobedient; that
schools and colleges were grown turbulent ; that Indians slighted their guardians, and negroes grew insolent to their masters.　But your letter[1] was the first

---

[1] This letter is not in the published volumes.　The para-
graph to which this is in answer runs as follows :　" I long to
hear that you have declared an independency.　And by the
way, in the new code of laws which I suppose it will be necessary to make, I desire you would remember the ladies, and

intimation that another tribe, more numerous and powerful than all the rest, were grown discontented.
This is rather too coarse a compliment, but you are so
saucy, I won't blot it out. Depend upon it, we know
better than to repeal our masculine systems. Although they are in full force, you know they are little more than theory. We dare not exert our power
in its full latitude. We are obliged to go fair and
softly, and, in practice, you know we are the subjects.
We have only the name of masters, and rather than
give up this, which would completely subject us to
the despotism of the petticoat, I hope, General Washington, and all our brave heroes would fight; I am
sure, every good politician would plot, as long as he
would against despotism, empire, monarchy, aristoc-
racy, oligarchy or ochlocracy. A fine story indeed!
I begin to think the ministry as deep as they are
wicked. After stirring up tories, land-jobbers, trim-
mers, bigots, Canadians, Indians, Negroes, Hano-
verians, Hessians, Russians, Irish Roman Catholics,
Scotch renegadoes, at last, they have stimulated
the ———— to demand new privileges and threaten to
rebel.

be more generous and favorable to them than your ancestors
were. Do not put such an unlimited power into the hands of
the husbands. Remember, all men would be tyrants, if they
could. If particular care and attention are not paid to the
ladies, we are determined to foment a rebellion, and will not
hold ourselves bound by any laws in which we have no voice
or representation."

LETTER L.

Philadelphia, 15 April, 1776.

I SEND you every newspaper that comes out, and I
send you, now and then, a few sheets of paper, but
this article is as scarce here, as with you.   I would
send a quire, if I could get a conveyance.

I write you now and then a line, as often as I can,
but I can tell you no news, but what I send in the
public papers.

We are waiting, it is said, for commissioners; a
messiah that will never come. This story of commissioners is as arrant an illusion as ever was hatched
in the brain of an enthusiast, a politician, or a maniac.
I have laughed at it, scolded at it, grieved at it, and I
don't know but I may, at an unguarded moment, have
rip'd at it.   But it is vain to reason against such de-
lusions.   1 was very sorry to see, in a letter from the
General, that he had been bubbled with it; and still
more, to see, in a letter from my sagacious friend,
W.[1] at Plymouth, that he was taken in too.

My opinion is, that the commissioners and the commission have been here, (I mean in America,) these
two months.   The Governors, Mandamus Councillors, Collectors and Comptrollers and Commanders of
the army and navy, I conjecture, compose the list,

[1] James Warren.

and their power is to receive submissions. But we are not in a very submissive mood. They will get no advantage of us. We shall go on to perfection, I believe. I have been very busy for some time; have written about ten sheets of paper, with my own hand, about some trifling affairs,[1] which I may mention some time or other — not now, for fear of accidents.

What will come of this labor, time will discover. I shall get nothing by it, I believe, because I never get anything by anything that I do. I am sure the public or posterity ought to get something. I believe my children will think I might as well have thought and labored a little, night and day, for their benefit. But I will not bear the reproaches of my children. I will tell them, that I studied and labored to procure a free constitution of government for them to solace themselves under, and if they do not prefer this to ample fortune, to ease and elegance, they are not my children, and I care not what becomes of them. They shall live upon thin diet, wear mean clothes, and work hard with cheerful hearts and free spirits, or they may be the children of the earth, or of no one, for me.

John has genius and so has Charles. Take care that they don't go astray. Cultivate their minds, inspire their little hearts, raise their wishes. Fix their attention upon great and glorious objects. Root out every little thing. Weed out every meanness. Make

---

[1] This probably alludes to the " Thoughts on Government," in the form of a letter to George Wythe, of Virginia — a paper that presents a sketch of the system which has since been generally adopted by the States of the Union.

them great and manly. Teach them to scorn injustice, ingratitude, cowardice and falsehood. Let them
revere nothing but religion, morality and liberty.

Abby and Tommy are not forgotten by me although I did not mention them before. The first, by
reason of her sex, requires a different education from
the two I have mentioned. Of this, you are the only
judge. I want to send each of my little pretty flock
some present or other. I have walked over this city
twenty times, and gaped at every shop, like a coun-
tryman, to find something, but could not. Ask every
one of them what they would choose to have, and
write it to me in your next letter. From this I shall
judge of their taste and fancy and discretion.

LETTER LI.

[Philadelphia], 23 April, 1776.

THIS is St. George's day, a festival celebrated by the
English, as St. Patrick's is by the Irish, St. David's
by the Welsh, and St. Andrew's by the Scotch. The
natives of Old England in this city, heretofore formed
a society, which they called St. George's club or St.
George's society. Upon the twenty-third of April,
annually, they had a great feast. But the Tories and
politics have made a schism in the society, so that one
part of them are to meet and dine at the City Tavern,

and the other at the Bunch of Grapes Israel Ja-
cobs's, and a third party go out of town. One set are
stanch Americans, another stanch Britons, and a
third, halfway men, neutral beings, moderate men,
prudent folks, for such is the division among men upon
all occasions and every question. This is the account
which I have from my barber, who is one of the society, and zealous on the side of America, and one of
the Philadelphia Associators.

This curious character of a barber, I have a great
inclination to draw, for your amusement. He is a little dapper fellow, short and small, but active and
lively. A tongue as fluent and voluble as you please,
wit at will, and a memory or an invention which never
leaves him at a loss for a story to tell you for your
entertainment. He has seen great company. He
has dressed hair and shaved faces at Bath, and at
Court. He is acquainted with several of the nobility
and gentry, particularly Sir William Meredith. He
married a girl, the daughter of a Quaker in this place,
of whom he tells many droll stories. He is a serjeant
in one of the companies of some battalion or other
here. He frequents, of evenings, a beer house kept by
one Weaver in the city, where he has many curious
disputes and adventures, and meets many odd characters.

I believe you will think me very idle to write you
so trifling a letter, upon so uninteresting a subject, at
a time when my country is fighting *pro aris et focis*.
But I assure you I am glad to chat with this barber,
while he is shaving and combing me, to divert myself

from less agreeable thoughts. He is so sprightly and good humoured, that he contributes, more than I could have imagined, to my comfort in this life. Burne has prepared a string of toasts for the club to drink to-day at Israel's.

The thirteen united colonies.

The free and independent States of America.

The Congress for the time being.

The American army and navy.

The Governor and Council of South Carolina, &c., &c., &c.

An happy election for the Whigs on the first of May, &c.

LETTER LII.

[Philadelphia], 28 April, 1776.

YESTERDAY I received two letters[1] from you from the 7th to the 14th of April. It gives me concern to think of the many cares you must have upon your mind. Your reputation as a farmer or anything else you undertake, I dare answer for. Your partner's character as a statesman is much more problematical.

As to my return, I have not a thought of it. Jour-

-----

[1] See the first of these in the collection by Mrs. Adams, Vol. I. p. 95.

neys of such a length are tedious, and expensive both
of time and money, neither of which is my own. I
hope to spend the next Christmas where I did the last,
and after that, I hope to be relieved; for by that time,
I shall have taken a pretty good trick at helm, whether
the vessel has been well steered or not. But if my
countrymen should insist upon my serving them another year, they must let me bring my whole family
with me. Indeed, I could keep house here with my
partner, four children and two servants as cheap as I
maintain myself here with two horses and a servant
at lodgings.

Instead of domestic felicity, I am destined to public
contentions. Instead of rural felicity, I must reconcile myself to the smoke and noise of a city. In the
place of private peace, I must be distracted with the
vexation of developing the deep intrigues of politicians, and must assist in conducting the arduous operations of war, and think myself well rewarded if my
private pleasure and interests are sacrificed, as they
ever have been and will be, to the happiness of
others.

You tell me, our Jurors refuse to serve, because the
writs are issued in the King's name. I am very glad
to hear that they discover so much sense and spirit.
I learn, from another letter, that the general court have
left out of their bills the year of his reign, and that
they are making a law, that the same name shall be
left out of all writs, commissions, and all law pro-
cesses. This is good news too. The same will be
the case in all the colonies, very soon.

You ask me, how I have done the winter past? I have not enjoyed so good health as last fall. But I have done complaining of anything. Of ill health, I have no right to complain, because it is given me by Heaven. Of meanness, of envy, of littleness, of—, of—, of—, I have reason and right to complain, but I have too much contempt to use that right. There is such a mixture of folly, littleness and knavery in this world, that I am weary of it, and although I behold it with unutterable contempt and indignation, yet the public good requires that I should take no notice of it by word or by letter. And to this public good I will conform.

You will see an account of the fleet in some of the papers I have sent you. I give you joy of the Admiral's success. I have vanity enough to take to myself a share in the merit of the American navy. It was always a measure that my heart was much engaged in, and I pursued it for a long time against the wind and tide, but at last obtained it.

Is there no way for two friendly souls to converse together although the bodies are four hundred miles off? Yes, by letter. But I want a better communication. I want to hear you think or to see your thoughts. The conclusion of your letter makes my heart throb, more than a cannonade would. You bid me burn your letters. But I must forget you first. In yours of April 14 you say, you miss our friend in the conveyance of your letters. Don't hesitate to write by the post. Seal well. Don't miss a single post. You take it for granted that I have particular

intelligence of everything from others, but I have not.
If any one wants a vote for a commission he vouch-
safes me a letter, but tells me very little news. I
have more particulars from you, than any one else.
Pray keep me constantly informed what ships are in
the harbor and what fortifications are going on. I
am quite impatient to hear of more vigorous measures
for fortifying Boston harbor. Not a moment should be
neglected. Every man ought to go down, as they did
after the battle of Lexington, and work until it is done.
I would willingly pay half a dozen hands myself, and
subsist them, rather than it should not be done immediately. It is of more importance than to raise corn.
You say enclosed is a prologue and a parody, but neither was enclosed. If you did not forget it, the letter
has been opened and the enclosures taken out. If the
small pox spreads, run me in debt. I received, a
post or two past, a letter from your uncle at Salem,
containing a most friendly and obliging invitation to
you and yours, to go and have the distemper at his
house, if it should spread. He has one or two in his
family to have it.

The writer of " Common Sense " and the " Forrester "
is the same person. His name is Paine, a gentleman
about two years ago from England, a man who, General Lee says, has genius in his eyes. The writer of
" Cassandra " is said to be Mr. James Cannon, a tutor in
the Philadelphia college. " Cato " is reported here to be
Doctor Smith — a match for Brattle. The oration
was an insolent performance. A motion was made to
thank the Orator, and ask a copy, but opposed with

great spirit and vivacity from every part of the room, and at last withdrawn, lest it should be rejected, as it certainly would have been, with indignation. The Orator then printed it himself, after leaving out or altering some offensive passages. This is one of the many irregular and extravagant characters of the age. I never heard one single person speak well of anything about him, but his abilities, which are generally allowed to be good. The appointment of him to make the oration was a great oversight and mistake.

The last act of Parliament has made so deep an impression upon people's minds, throughout the colonies, it is looked upon as the last stretch of oppression, that we are hastening rapidly to great events. Governments will be up, everywhere, before midsummer and an end to royal style, titles and authority. Such mighty revolutions make a deep impression on the minds of men, and set many violent passions at work. Hope, fear, joy, sorrow, love, hatred, malice, envy, revenge, jealousy, ambition, avarice, resentment, gratitude, and every other passion, feeling, sentiment, principle and imagination were never in more lively exercise than they are now from Florida to Canada inclusively. May God in his providence overrule the whole for the good of mankind. It requires more serenity of temper, a deeper understanding and more courage than fell to the lot of Marlborough to ride in this whirlwind.

LETTER LIII.

[Philadelphia], 12 May, 1776.

YOURS of 21 April came to hand yesterday. I send you regularly every newspaper, and write as often as I can; but I feel more skittish about writing than I did, because, since the removal of head-quarters to New York, we have no express, and very few individual travellers; and the post I am not quite confident in; however, I shall write as I can.

What shall I do with my office? I want to resign it for a thousand reasons. Would you advise me?

There has been a gallant battle in Delaware river between the galleys and two men of war, the Roebuck and Liverpool, in which the men of war came off second best; which has diminished, in the minds of the people on both sides of the river, the terror of a man of war.

I long to hear a little of my private affairs; yet I dread it too, because I know you must be perplexed and distressed. I wish it was in my power to relieve you. It gives me great pleasure to learn, that our rulers are, at last, doing something towards the fortification of Boston. But I am inexpressibly chagrined to find that the enemy is fortifying on George's Island. I never shall be easy, until they are completely driven out of that harbor, and effectually prevented from ever getting in again. As you are a politician and now

elected into an important office, that of judgess of the
Tory ladies, which will give you, naturally, an influence with your sex, I hope you will be instant, in season and out of season, in exhorting them to use
their influence with the gentlemen, to fortify upon
George's Island, Lovell's, Pettick's, Long, or wherever
else it is proper.   Send down fire ships and rafts, and
burn to ashes those pirates.   I am out of patience with
the languid, lethargic councils of the province, at such
a critical, important moment, puzzling their heads
about twopenny fees, and confession bills, and what
not, when the harbor of Boston is defenceless.   If I
was there, I should storm and thunder like Demos-
thenes, or scold like a tooth-drawer.   Do ask Mr.
Wibird and Mr. Weld and Mr. Taft to preach about
it.   I am ashamed, vexed, angry to the last degree.
Our people, by their torpitude, have invited the enemy to come to Boston again, and I fear they will have
the civility and politeness to accept the invitation.

Your uncle has never answered my letter.   Thank
the Doctor, he has written me a most charming letter,
full of intelligence, and very sensible and useful remarks.   I will pay the debt, as far as my circumstances will admit, and as soon.   But I hope my friends
will not wait for regular returns from me.   I have not
yet left off pitying " the fifty or sixty men ; " and if
my friends knew all that I do, they would pity too.

Betsey Smith, lazy hussy, has not written me a
line a great while.   I wish she was married ; then
she would have some excuse.   Duty to papa.   Love
to all.   How is the family over against the church ?

LETTER LIV.

[Philadelphia], 17 May, 1776.

I HAVE this morning heard Mr. Duffield, upon the signs
of the times. He ran a parallel between the case of
Israel, and that of America; and between the conduct of Pharaoh, and that of George. Jealousy that
the Israelites would throw off the government of
Egypt made him issue his edict, that the midwives
should cast the children into the river, and the other
edict, that the men should make a large revenue of
bricks without straw. He concluded, that the course
of events indicated strongly the design of Providence,
that we should be separated from Great Britain, &c.

Is it not a saying of Moses, " who am I, that I
should go in and out before this great people ? "
When I consider the great events which are passed,
and those greater which are rapidly advancing, and
that I may have been instrumental in touching some
springs, and turning some small wheels, which have
had and will have such effects, I feel an awe upon my
mind, which is not easily described. Great Britain
has at last driven America to the last step, a complete separation from her ; a total absolute independence, not only of her Parliament, but of her crown,
for such is the amount of the resolve of the 15th.[1] Con-

---

[1] " On the sixth of May, Mr. Adams offered in committee
of the whole, a resolve that the colonies should form govern-

federation among ourselves, or alliances with foreign nations are not necessary to a perfect separation from Britain. That is effected by extinguishing all authority under the crown, Parliament, and nation, as the resolution for instituting governments has done, to all intents and purposes. Confederation will be necessary for our internal concord, and alliances may be so for our external defence.

I have reasons to believe that no colony, which shall assume a government under the people, will give it up. There is something very unnatural and odious in a government a thousand leagues off. A whole government of our own choice, managed by persons whom we love, revere, and can confide in, has charms in it, for which men will fight. Two young gentlemen from South Carolina in this city, who were in Charlestown when their new constitution was promulgated, and when their new Governor and Council and Assem-

ments independent of the crown. The shape in which this proposition was adopted on the tenth, was a recommendation to the respective assemblies and conventions of the united colonies, where no government sufficient to the exigencies of their affairs had been yet established, to adopt such government as might in their opinion best conduce to the safety and happiness of their constituents in particular, and America in general." Biography of the Signers to the Declaration of Independence. Article, "John Adams," Vol. viii. p. 268. This resolution was passed on the 10th of May, accompanied with another appointing Mr. Adams, Mr. Rutledge and Mr. R. H. Lee, a committee to prepare a preamble. This committee accordingly reported the draught of a preamble, which was agreed to on the 15th, the date named in this letter. Journals of Congress, Vol. ii. pp. 166, 174.

bly walked out in procession, attended by the guards, company of cadets, light horse, &c., told me, that they were beheld by the people with transports and tears of joy. The people gazed at them with a kind of rapture. They both told me, that the reflection, that these were gentlemen whom they all loved, esteemed and revered, gentlemen of their own choice, whom they could trust, and whom they could displace, if any of them should behave amiss, affected them so, that they could not help crying. They say, their people will never give up this government. One of these gentlemen is a relation of yours, a Mr. Smith, son of Mr. Thomas Smith. I shall give him this letter or another to you.

A privateer fitted out here by Colonel Roberdeau and Major Bayard since our resolves for privateering, I am this moment informed, has taken a valuable prize. This is encouragement at the beginning.

In one or two of your letters, you remind me to think of you as I ought. Be assured, there is not an hour of the day, in which I don't think of you as I ought, that is, with every sentiment of tenderness, esteem and admiration.

[Philadelphia], 22 May, 1776.

WHEN a man is seated in the midst of forty people, some of whom are talking, and others whispering, it is not easy to think what is proper to write. I shall send you the newspapers, which will inform you of public affairs, and the particular flickerings of parties in this colony. I am happy to learn from your letter, that a flame is at last raised among the people, for the fortification of the harbor. Whether Nantasket or Point Alderton would be proper posts to be taken, I can't say. But I would fortify every place which is proper, and which cannon could be obtained for. Generals Gates and Mifflin are now here. General Washington will be here to-morrow, when we shall consult and deliberate concerning the operations of the ensuing campaign.

We have dismal accounts from Europe of the preparations against us. This summer will be very important to us. We shall have a severe trial of our patience, fortitude and perseverance. But I hope we shall do valiantly, and tread down our enemies.

I have some thoughts of petitioning the General Court for leave to bring my family here. I am a lonely, forlorn creature here. It used to be some comfort to me, that I had a servant and some horses. They composed a sort of family for me. But now, there is not one creature here, that I seem to have any kind of relation to. It is a cruel reflection, which very often comes across me, that I should be separated so far from those babes, whose education and welfare lie so near my heart. But greater misfortunes than these must not divert us from superior duties.

Your sentiments of the duties we owe to our country are such as become the best of women and the best of men. Among all the disappointments and perplexities which have fallen to my share in life, nothing has contributed so much to support my mind, as the choice blessing of a wife, whose capacity enabled her to comprehend, and whose pure virtue obliged her to approve the views of her husband. This has been the cheering consolation of my heart in my most solitary, gloomy and disconsolate hours. In this remote situation, I am deprived in a great measure of this comfort. Yet I read and read again your charming letters, and they serve me, in some faint degree, as a substitute for the company and conversation of the writer. I want to take a walk with you in the garden, to go over to the common, the plain, the meadow. I want to take Charles in one hand and Tom in the other, and walk with you, Abby on your right hand, and John upon my left, to view the corn fields, the orchards, &c.

Alas, poor imagination! how faintly and imperfectly do you supply the want of originality and reality. But instead of these pleasing scenes of domestic life, I hope you will not be disturbed with the alarms of war. I hope, yet I fear.

LETTER LVI.

[Philadelphia], 27 May, 1776.

I HAVE three[1] of your favors before me. One of
May 7, another of May 9, and a third of May 14th.
The last has given me relief from many anxieties. It
relates wholly to private affairs, and contains such an
account of wise and prudent management, as makes
me very happy. I begin to be jealous, that our neigh-
bors will think affairs more discreetly conducted in my
absence, than at any other time. Whether your suspicions concerning a letter under a marble cover are
just or not, it is best to say little about it. It is a
hasty,[2] hurried thing, and of no great consequence,
calculated for a meridian at a great distance from
New England. If it has done no good, it will do
no harm. It has contributed to set people thinking
upon the subject, and in this respect has answered its
end. The manufacture of governments having, since
the publication of that letter, been as much talked of,
as that of saltpetre was before.

I rejoice at your account of the spirit of fortification, and the good effects of it. I hope, by this time,
you are in a tolerable posture of defence. The inhabitants of Boston have done themselves great honor
by their laudable zeal, the clergymen, especially.

---

[1] Letters of Mrs. Adams, Vol. I. p. 99. The letter of the
14th, being wholly of a private nature, is not published.
[2] "Thoughts on Government," already referred to.

I think you shine as a stateswoman of late, as well as a farmeress. Pray where do you get your maxims of state ? They are very apropos. I am much obliged to Judge Cushing and his lady for their polite visit to you. I should be very happy to see him, and converse with him about many things, but cannot hope for that pleasure very soon. The affairs of America are in so critical a state, such great events are struggling into birth that I must not quit this station at this time. Yet I dread the melting heats of a Philadelphia summer, and know not how my frail constitution will endure it. Such constant care, such incessant application of mind, drinking up and exhausting the finer spirits, upon which life and health so essentially depend, will wear away a stronger man than I am. Yet I will not shrink from this danger or this toil. While my health shall be such, that I can discharge, in any tolerable manner, the duties of this important post, I will not desert it.

I am pleased to hear that the superior court is to sit at Ipswich in June. This will contribute to give stability to the government, I hope, in all its branches. But I presume other steps will be taken for this purpose. A Governor, and Lieutenant Governor, I hope, will be chosen, and the Constitution a little more fixed. I hope too, that the council will, this year, be more full, and augmented by the addition of good men. I hope Mr. Bowdoin will be Governor, if his health will permit, and Doctor Winthrop, Lieutenant Governor. These are wise, learned and prudent men. The first has a great fortune and wealthy connexions. The other has the advantage of a name and family which is much reverenced, besides his personal abilities and virtues, which are very great.

Our friend,[1] I sincerely hope, will not refuse his appointment. For although I have ever thought that bench should be filled from the bar, and once labored successfully to effect it, yet as the gentlemen have seen fit to decline, I know of no one who would do more honor to the station, than my friend. None would be so agreeable to me, whether I am to sit by him or before him. I suppose it must be disagreeable to him and his lady, because he loves to be upon his farm, and they both love to be together. But you must tell them of a couple of their friends, who are as fond of living together, who are obliged to sacrifice their rural amusements and domestic happiness to the requisitions of the public.

The Generals, Washington, Gates and Mifflin are all here, and we shall derive spirit, unanimity and vigor from their presence and advice. I hope you will have some general officers at Boston soon. I am, with constant wishes and prayers for your health and prosperity, forever yours.

[1] James Warren.

LETTER LVII.

[Philadelphia], 2 June, 1776.

YESTERDAY I dined with Captain Richards, the gentleman who made me the present of the brass pistols.
We had cherries, strawberries and green peas in plenty.
The fruits are three weeks earlier here, than with
you.   Indeed, they are a fortnight earlier on the east,
than on the west side of Delaware river.   We have
had green peas this week past, but they were brought
over the river, from New Jersey, to this market.
There are none grown in the city, or on the west side
of the river yet.   The reason is, the soil of New Jersey is a warm sand ; that of Pennsylvania a cold clay.
So much for peas and berries.

Now for something of more importance.   In all the
correspondence I have maintained, during a course
of twenty years, at least, that I have been a writer of
letters, I never kept a single copy.   This negligence
and inaccuracy has been a great misfortune to me on
many occasions.   I have now purchased a folio book,
in the first page of which, excepting one blank leaf, I
am writing this letter, and intend to write all my letters to you in it, from this time forward.   This will
be an advantage to me in several respects.   In the
first place, I shall write more deliberately.   In the
second place, I shall be able, at all times, to review
what I have written.   Third, I shall know how often

I write. Fourth, I shall discover by this means, whether any of my letters to you miscarry. If it were possible for me to find a conveyance, I would send you such another blank book as a present, that you might begin the practice at the same time, for I really think that your letters are much better worth preserving than mine. Your daughter and sons will very soon write so good hands, that they will copy the letters for you from your book, which will improve them, at the same time that it relieves you.

LETTER LVIII.

[Philadelphia], 16 June, 1776.

YESTERDAY was to me a lucky day, as it brought me two letters from you. One dated May 27, and the other June 3d. Don't be concerned about me, if it happens now and then, that you don't hear from me for some weeks together. If anything should injure my health materially, you will soon hear of it. But I thank God, I am in much better health than I expected to be. But this cannot last long under the load that I carry. When it becomes too great for my strength, I shall ask leave to lay it down, and come home. But I will hold it out a good while yet, if I can.

I wish our uncle [1] had as much ambition, as he has

[1] Norton Quincy was elected by the first provincial Con-

virtue and ability. A deficiency of ambition is as
criminal and injurious as an excess of it. Tell him
I say so. How shall we contrive to make so wise and
good a man ambitious? Is it not a sin to be so modest? Ask him how he can answer it? Thanks for
your quotation from Sully. It is extremely apropos.
I am very glad you are so well provided with help.
Give my respects to Mr. Belcher and his family. Tell
him I am obliged to him for his kind care of the farm.
I wish I could go out with him, and see the business go
on, but I can't. Thank your father and my mother
for their kind remembrance of me. Return my duty
to both. Charles's young heroism charms me. Kiss
him. Poor Mugford,[1] yet glorious Mugford! How
beautiful and sublime it is to die for one's country!
What a fragrant memory remains!

The rumor you heard of General Gates will prove
premature. I endeavoured both here and with the
General to have it so,[2] and should have succeeded, if
it had not been for the loss of General Thomas. Cruel
small pox! worse than the sword! But now, I fear

gress of Massachusetts, in 1774, one of the nine members of
the committee of safety — but declined serving in that or in
any other public capacity throughout his life.

Captain Mugford distinguished himself by the capture,
within sight of the British fleet, of the ship Hope, from Cork,
laden with gunpowder and other military stores. His vessel
was afterwards attacked by thirteen boats from the men of
war. They were beaten off with great loss, but he, alone of
the American side, fell in the skirmish. See Gordon's History,
Vol. ii. p. 263, and Bradford's History of Massachusetts, Vol. ii.
p. 109.

[2] That he should have the command of Boston.

we must part with Gates for the sake of Canada. Mrs.
Montgomery is a lady, like all the family, of refined
sentiments and elegant accomplishments. Her letter,
as you quote it, is very pathetic. I rejoice to hear
that the enemy have not fortified ; and hope they will
not be suffered to attempt it.

Don't think about my clothes. I do well enough
in that respect. As to your house at Boston, do with
it as you please. Sell it, if you will, but not for a
farthing less than it cost me. Let it, if you please,
but take care who your tenant is, both of his prudence to preserve the house, and his ability to pay the
rent.

I send you all the news in the papers. Great things
are on the tapis.[1] These throes will usher in the
birth of a fine boy. We have no thoughts of removing from hence. There is no occasion for it.

LETTER LIX.

Philadelphia, 26 June, 1776.

I HAVE written so seldom to you, that I am really
grieved at the recollection. I wrote you a few lines

---

[1] A manifest allusion to the measures in progress for a Declaration of Independence. Resolutions had been moved on
the 7th. and a committee for preparing the Declaration had
been appointed on the 11th, of which Committee, it is well
known, Mr. Adams was a member.

June 2, and a few more June 16. These are all that I have written to you, since this month began. It has been the busiest month that ever I saw. I have found time to enclose all the newspapers, which I hope you will receive in due time.

Our misfortunes in Canada are enough to melt a heart of stone. The small pox is ten times more terrible than Britons, Canadians and Indians, together. This was the cause of our precipitate retreat from Quebec. This the cause of our disgraces at the Cedars. I don't mean that this was all. There has been want approaching to famine, as well as pestilence. And these discouragements have so disheartened our officers, that none of them seem to act with prudence and firmness. But these reverses of fortune don't discourage me. It was natural to expect them, and we ought to be prepared in our minds for greater changes, and more melancholy scenes still. It is an animating cause, and brave spirits are not subdued with difficulties.

Amidst all our gloomy prospects in Canada, we receive some pleasure from Boston. I congratulate you on your victory over your enemies in the harbor. This has long lain near my heart, and it gives me great pleasure to think that what was so much wished is accomplished. I hope our people will now make the lower harbor impregnable, and never again suffer the flag of a tyrant to fly within any part of it.

The Congress have been pleased to give me more business than I am qualified for, and more than, I fear, I can go through with safety to my health. They have established a board of war and ordnance, and made me President of it,[1] an honor to which I never aspired, a trust to which I feel myself vastly unequal. But I am determined to do as well as I can, and make industry supply, in some degree, the place of abilities and experience. The Board sits every morning and every evening. This with constant attendance in Congress will so entirely engross my time, that I fear, I shall not be able to write you so often as I have. But I will steal time to write to you.

The small pox! the small pox! what shall we do with it? I could almost wish that an inoculating Hospital was opened in every town in New England, It is some small consolation that the scoundrel savages have taken a large dose of it. They plundered the baggage and stripped off the clothes of our men who had the small pox out full upon them at the Cedars.

---

[1] Besides his position on the Committee, appointed on the 11th of June, to draught a Declaration of Independence, Mr. Adams had been chosen on the next day, one of a Committee to prepare a plan of treaties to be proposed to foreign powers, and on the day after that, Chairman of the board of war. Journals of Congress, Vol. ii. pp. 207, 208, 211.

LETTER LX.

Philadelphia, 3 July, 1776.

YOUR favor[1] of 17 June, dated at Plymouth, was handed me by yesterday's post. I was much pleased to find that you had taken a journey to Plymouth, to see your friends, in the long absence of one, whom you may wish to see. The excursion will be an amusement, and will serve your health. How happy would it have made me to have taken this journey with you!

I was informed, a day or two before the receipt of your letter, that you was gone to Plymouth, by Mrs. Polly Palmer, who was obliging enough, in your absence, to send me the particulars of the expedition to the lower harbor against the men of war. Her narration is executed with a precision and perspicuity, which would have become the pen of an accomplished historian.

I am very glad you had so good an opportunity of seeing one of our little American men of war. Many ideas new to you must have presented themselves in such a scene; and you will in future better understand the relations of sea engagements.

I rejoice extremely at Dr. Bulfinch's petition to open a Hospital. But I hope the business will be

---

[1] Letters of Mrs. Adams, Vol. I. p. 102.

done upon a larger scale. I hope that one Hospital will be licensed in every county, if not in every town. I am happy to find you resolved to be with the children in the first class. Mr. Whitney and Mrs. Katy Quincy are cleverly through inoculation in this city.

The information you give me, of our friend's refusing his appointment, has given me much pain, grief and anxiety. I believe I shall be obliged to follow his example. I have not fortune enough to support my family, and, what is of more importance, to support the dignity of that exalted station. It is too high and lifted up for me, who delight in nothing so much as retreat, solitude, silence and obscurity. In private life, no one has a right to censure me for following my own inclinations in retirement, simplicity and frugality. In public life, every man has a right to remark as he pleases. At least he thinks so.

Yesterday, the greatest question was decided, which ever was debated in America, and a greater, perhaps, never was nor will be decided among men. A Resolution was passed without one dissenting Colony "that these United Colonies are, and of right ought to be, free and independent States, and as such they have, and of right ought to have, full power to make war, conclude peace, establish commerce and to do all other acts and things which other States may rightfully do." You will see, in a few days, a Declaration setting forth the causes which have impelled us to this mighty revolution, and the reasons which will justify it in the sight of God and man. A plan of confederation will be taken up in a few days.

When I look back to the year 1761 and recollect the argument concerning writs of assistance in the superior court, which I have hitherto considered as the commencement of this controversy between Great Britain and America, and run through the whole period, from that time to this, and recollect the series of political events, the chain of causes and effects, I am surprised at the suddenness, as well as greatness of this revolution. Britain has been filled with folly, and America with wisdom; at least, this is my judgment. Time must determine. It is the will of Heaven that the two countries should be sundered forever. It may be the will of Heaven that America shall suffer calamities still more wasting, and distresses yet more dreadful. If this is to be the case, it will have this good effect at least. It will inspire us with many virtues, which we have not, and correct many errors, follies and vices which threaten to disturb, dishonor, and destroy us. The furnace of affliction produces refinement in states as well as individuals. And the new Governments we are assuming in every part will require a purification from our vices, and an augmentation of our virtues, or they will be no blessings. The people will have unbounded power, and the people are extremely addicted to corruption and venality, as well as the great. But I must submit all my hopes and fears to an overruling providence, in which, unfashionable as the faith may be, I firmly believe.

LETTER LXI.

Philadelphia, 3 July, 1776.

HAD a Declaration of Independency been made seven months ago, it would have been attended with many great and glorious effects. We might, before this hour, have formed alliances with foreign states. We should have mastered Quebec, and been in possession of Canada. You will perhaps wonder how such a declaration would have influenced our affairs in Canada, but if I could write with freedom, I could easily convince you that it would, and explain to you the manner how. Many gentlemen in high stations and of great influence, have been duped by the ministerial bubble of Commissioners to treat. And in real, sincere expectation of this event, which they so fondly wished, they have been slow and languid in promoting measures for the reduction of that province. Others there are in the Colonies who really wished that our enterprise in Canada would be defeated, that the Colonies might be brought into danger and distress between two fires, and be thus induced to submit. Others really wished to defeat the expedition to Canada, lest the conquest of it should elevate the minds of the people too much to hearken to those terms of reconciliation, which, they believed, would be offered us. These jarring views, wishes and designs occasioned an opposition to many salutary measures, which were proposed for the support of that expedition, and caused obstructions, embarrassments, and studied delays, which have finally lost us the province.

All these causes however in conjunction would not have disappointed us, if it had not been for a misfortune which could not be foreseen, and perhaps, could not have been prevented — I mean the prevalence of the small pox among our troops. This fatal pestilence completed our destruction. It is a frown of providence upon us, which we ought to lay to heart.

But, on the other hand, the delay of this Declaration to this time has many great advantages attending it. The hopes of reconciliation, which were fondly entertained by multitudes of honest and well meaning, though weak and mistaken people, have been gradually and, at last, totally extinguished. Time has been given for the whole people maturely to consider the great question of independence, and to ripen their judgment, dissipate their fears, and allure their hopes, by discussing it in newspapers and pamphlets, by debating it in assemblies, conventions, committees of safety and inspection, in town and county meetings, as well as in private conversations, so that the whole people, in every colony of the thirteen, have now adopted it as their own act. This will cement the union, and avoid those heats, and perhaps convulsions, which might have been occasioned by such a Declaration, six months ago.

But the day is past. The second[1] day of July, 1776, will be the most memorable epocha in the history of America. I am apt to believe that it will be celebrated by succeeding generations as the great anniversary Festival. It ought to be commemorated, as the day of deliverance, by solemn acts of devotion to God Almighty. It ought to be solemnized with pomp and parade, with shows, games, sports, guns, bells, bonfires and illuminations, from one end

---

[1] The practice has been to celebrate the 4th of July, the day upon which the form of the declaration of Independence was agreed to, rather than the 2d, the day upon which the resolution, making that declaration, was determined upon by the Congress. A friend of Mr. Adams, who had during his lifetime an opportunity to read the two letters dated on the 3d, was so much struck with them, that he procured the liberty to publish them. But thinking, probably, that a slight alteration would better fit them for the taste of the day, and gain for them a higher character for prophecy, than if printed as they were, he obtained leave to put together only the most remarkable paragraphs, and make one letter out of the two. He then changed the date from the 3d to the 5th, and the word second to fourth, and published it, the public being made aware of these alterations. In this form, and as connected with the anniversary of our National Independence, these letters have, ever since, enjoyed great popularity. The Editor at first entertained some doubt of the expediency of making a variation by printing them in their original shape. But upon considering the matter well, his determination to adhere, in all cases, to the text, prevailed. If any injury to the reputation of Mr. Adams for prophecy should ensue, it will be greater in the form than in the substance, and will not be, perhaps, without compensation in the restoration of the unpublished portion.

of this continent to the other, from this time forward, forevermore.

You will think me transported with enthusiasm, but I am not. I am well aware of the toil, and blood, and treasure, that it will cost us to maintain this Declaration, and support and defend these States. Yet, through all the gloom, I can see the rays of ravishing light and glory. I can see that the end is more than worth all the means. And that posterity will triumph in that day's transaction, even although we should rue it, which I trust in God we shall not.

LETTER LXII.

Philadelphia, 7 July, 1776.

I HAVE, this moment, folded up a magazine and an Evening Post, and sent them off by an express, who could not wait for me to write a single line. It always goes to my heart, to send off a packet of pamphlets and newspapers, without a letter, but it sometimes unavoidably happens, and I suppose you had rather receive a pamphlet or newspaper, than nothing.

The design of our enemy now seems to be, a powerful invasion of New York and New Jersey. The Halifax fleet and army is arrived, and another fleet and army under Lord Howe is expected to join them. We are making great preparations to meet them, by marching the militia of Maryland, Pennsylvania and New Jersey down to the scene of action, and have made large requisitions upon New England. I hope, for the honor of New England, and the salvation of America, our people will not be backward in marching to New York. We must maintain and defend that important post, at all events. If the enemy get possession there, it will cost New England very dear. There is no danger of the small pox at New York. It is carefully kept out of the city and the army. I hope that your brother and mine too will go into the service of their country at this critical period of its distress.

Our army at Crown Point is an object of wretchedness enough to fill a humane mind with horror; disgraced, defeated, discontented, dispirited, diseased, naked, undisciplined, eaten up with vermin, no clothes, beds, blankets, no medicines, no victuals, but salt pork and flour. A chaplain from that army preached a sermon here the other day from " Cursed is he, that doeth the work of the Lord, deceitfully." I knew, better than he did, who the persons were, who deserved these curses. But I could not help myself, nor my poor country, any more than he. I hope that measures will be taken to cleanse the army at Crown Point from the small pox, and that other measures will be taken in New England, by tolerating and encouraging inoculation, to render that distemper less terrible.

I am solicitous to hear what figure our new superior court made in their eastern circuit. What business they did? whether the grand juries and petit juries were sworn? whether they tried any criminals, or any civil actions? how the people were affected at the appearance of Courts again? how the judges were treated? whether with respect or cold neglect, &c. Every colony upon the continent will soon be in the same situation. They are erecting governments as fast as children build cob-houses; but, I conjecture, they will hardly throw them down again so soon.

The practice we have hitherto been in, of ditching round about our enemies, will not always do. We must learn to use other weapons than the pick and the spade. Our armies must be disciplined, and learn to fight. I have the satisfaction to reflect that our Massachusetts people, when they have been left to themselves, have been constantly fighting and skirmishing, and always with success. I wish the same valor, prudence and spirit had been discovered every where.

LETTER LXIII.

Philadelphia, 7 July, 1776.

IT is worth the while of a person, obliged to write as much as I do, to consider the varieties of style. The epistolary is essentially different from the oratorical and the historical style. Oratory abounds with figures. History is simple, but grave, majestic and formal. Letters, like conversation, should be free, easy, and familiar. Simplicity and familiarity are the characteristics of this kind of writing. Affectation is as disagreeable in a letter, as in conversation, and therefore, studied language, premeditated method and sublime sentiments are not expected in a letter. Notwithstanding which, the sublime as well as the beautiful, and the novel, may naturally enough appear, in familiar letters among friends. Among the ancients there are two illustrious examples of the epistolary style, Cicero and Pliny, whose letters present you with models of fine writing, which have borne the criticism of almost two thousand years. In these you see the sublime, the beautiful, the novel and the pathetic, conveyed in as much simplicity, ease, freedom and familiarity, as language is capable of.

Let me request you to turn over the leaves of the Preceptor to a letter of Pliny the younger, in which he has transmitted to these days the history of his uncle's philosophical curiosity, his heroic courage and his melancholy catastrophe. Read it, and say, whether it is possible to write a narrative of facts in a better manner. It is copious and particular in selecting the circumstances most natural, remarkable and affecting. There is not an incident omitted, which ought to have been remembered, nor one inserted that is not worth remembrance. It gives you an idea of the scene, as distinct and perfect, as if a painter had drawn it to the life before your eyes. It interests your passions as much as if you had been an eye-witness of the whole transaction. Yet there are no figures or art used. All is as simple, natural, easy and familiar as if the story had been told in conversation, without a moment's premeditation.

Pope and Swift have given the world a collection of their letters; but I think, in general, they fall short, in the epistolary way, of their own eminence in poetry and other branches of literature. Very few of their letters have ever engaged much of my attention. Gay's letter concerning the pair of lovers killed by lightning, is worth more than the whole collection, in point of simplicity and elegance of composition, and as a genuine model of the epistolary style. There is a book, which I wish you owned, I mean Rollin's Belles Lettres, in which the variations of style are explained.

Early youth is the time to learn the arts and sciences, and especially to correct the ear and the imagination, by forming a style. I wish you would think of forming the taste and judgment of your child-ren now, before any unchaste sounds have fastened on their ears, and before any affectation or vanity is settled on their minds, upon the pure principles of nature. Music is a great advantage; for style de-pends, in part, upon a delicate ear. The faculty of writing is attainable by art, practice and habit only. The sooner, therefore, the practice begins, the more likely it will be to succeed. Have no mercy upon an affected phrase, any more than an affected air, gait, dress or manners.

Your children have capacities equal to any thing. There is a vigor in the understanding and a spirit and fire in the temper of every one of them, which is capable of ascending the heights of art, science, trade, war or politics. They should be set to compose descriptions of scenes and objects, and narrations of facts and events. Declamations upon topics and other exercises of various sorts should be prescribed to them. Set a child to form a description of a battle, a storm, a siege, a cloud, a mountain, a lake, a city, a harbor, a country seat, a meadow, a forest, or almost any thing that may occur to your thoughts. Set him to compose a narration of all the little incidents and events of a day, a journey, a ride or a walk. In this way a taste will be formed, and a facility of writing acquired.

For myself, as I never had a regular tutor, I never studied any thing methodically, and consequently, never was completely accomplished in any thing. But, as I am conscious of my own deficiency in these respects, I should be the less pardonable, if I neglected the education of my children. In grammar, rhetoric, logic, my education was imperfect, because immethodical. Yet I have perhaps read more upon these arts, and considered them in a more extensive view, than some others.

[Philadelphia], 10 July, 1776.

You will see, by the newspapers, which I, from time to time, enclose, with what rapidity the colonies proceed in their political manœuvres. How many calamities might have been avoided, if these measures had been taken twelve months ago, or even no longer ago than last December?

The colonies to the south are pursuing the same maxims which have heretofore governed those to the north. In constituting their new governments, their plans are remarkably popular, more so than I could ever have imagined; even more popular than the " Thoughts on Government ; " and in the choice of their rulers, capacity, spirit, and zeal in the cause supply the place of fortune, family, and every other consideration which used to have weight with mankind. My friend Archibald Bullock, Esquire, is Governor of Georgia. John Rutledge, Esquire, is Governor of South Carolina. Patrick Henry, Esquire, is Governor of Virginia, &c. Dr. Franklin will be Governor of Pennsylvania. The new members of this city are all in this taste, chosen because of their inflexible zeal for independence. All the old members left out because they opposed independence, or at least were lukewarm about it. Dickinson, Morris, Allen, all fallen, like grass before the scythe, notwithstanding all their

vast advantages in point of fortune, family and abilities. I am inclined to think, however, and to wish
that these gentlemen may be restored at a fresh election, because, although mistaken in some points, they
are good characters, and their great wealth and numerous connexions will contribute to strengthen America, and cement her union.

I wish I were at perfect liberty to portray before
you all these characters in their genuine lights, and
to explain to you the course of political changes in
this province. It would give you a great idea of the
spirit and resolution of the people, and show you, in a
striking point of view, the deep roots of American independence in all the colonies. But it is not prudent
to commit to writing such free speculations in the
present state of things. Time, which takes away the
veil, may lay open the secret springs of this surprising
revolution. But I find, although the colonies have dif-
fered in religion, laws, customs and manners, yet
in the great essentials of society and government,
they are all alike.

LETTER LXV.

Philadelphia, 11 July, 1776.

You seem to be situated in the place of greatest
tranquillity and security of any upon the continent.
I may be mistaken in this particular, and an armament may have invaded your neighborhood, before

now. But we have no intelligence of any such
design, and all that we now know of the motions,
plans, operations and designs of the enemy, indicates
the contrary. It is but just that you should have a
little rest, and take a little breath.

I wish I knew whether your brother and mine have
enlisted in the army, and what spirit is manifested by
our militia for marching to New York and Crown
point. The militia of Maryland, New Jersey, Pennsylvania and the lower counties are marching with
much alacrity, and a laudable zeal to take care of
Howe and his army at Staten Island. The army in
New York is in high spirits, and seems determined to give the enemy a serious reception. The
unprincipled and unfeeling and unnatural inhabitants
of Staten Island are cordially receiving the enemy,
and, deserters say, have engaged to take arms.
They are an ignorant, cowardly pack of scoundrels.
Their numbers are small, and their spirit less.

It is sometime since I received any letter from you.
The Plymouth one was the last. You must write
me, every week, by the post, if it is but a few lines.
It gives me many spirits. I design to write to the
General Court requesting a dismission, or at least,
a furlough. I think to propose that they choose four
more members, or, at least, three more, that so, we
may attend here in rotation. Two or three or four
may be at home at a time, and the Colony properly
represented notwithstanding. Indeed, while the Congress were employed in political regulations, forming
the sentiments of the people of the Colonies into

some consistent system, extinguishing the remainders of authority under the crown, and gradually erecting and strengthening governments under the authority of the people, turning their thoughts upon the principles of polity and the forms of government, framing constitutions for the Colonies separately, and a limited and a defined Confederacy for the United Colonies, and in some other measures, which I do not choose to mention particularly, but which are now determined, or near the point of determination, I flattered myself that I might have been of some little use here. But now, these matters will be soon completed, and very little business will be to be done here, but what will be either military or commercial; branches of knowledge and business for which hundreds of others in our province are much better qualified than I am. I shall therefore request my masters to relieve me.

I am not a little concerned about my health, which seems to have been providentially preserved to me, much beyond my expectations. But I begin to feel the disagreeable effects of unremitting attention to business for so long a time, and a want of exercise, and the bracing quality of my native air; so that I have the utmost reason to fear an irreparable injury to my constitution, if I do not obtain a little relaxation. The fatigues of war are much less destructive to health, than the painful, laborious attention to debates, and to writing, which drinks up the spirits and consumes the strength.

I am, &c.

LETTER LXVI.

Philadelphia, 15 July, 1776.

My very deserving friend, Mr. Gerry, sets off tomorrow for Boston, worn out of health, by the fatigues of this station. He is an excellent man, and an active, able statesman. I hope he will soon return hither. I am sure I should be glad to return with him, but I cannot. I must wait to have the guard relieved.

There is a most amiable, laudable and gallant spirit prevailing in these middle colonies. The militia turn out in great numbers, and in high spirits, in New Jersey, Pennsylvania, Maryland and Delaware, so that we hope to resist Howe and his myrmidons.

Independence is, at last, unanimously agreed to in the New York Convention. You will see, by the newspapers enclosed, what is going forward in Virginia and Maryland and New Jersey. Farewell! farewell! infatuated, besotted, step-dame. I have not time to add more, than that I receive letters from you but seldom of late. Tomorrow's post, I hope, will bring me some. So I hoped of last Saturday's and last Tuesday's.

Ever Yours.

LETTER LXVII.

Philadelphia, 20 July, 1776.

I CANNOT omit the opportunity of writing you a line by this post. This letter, will, I suppose, find you, in some degree or other, under the influence of the small pox. The air is of very great importance. I don't know your physician, but I hope he won't deprive you of air, more than is necessary.

We had yesterday an express from General Lee in Charleston, South Carolina, with an account of a brilliant little action between the armament under Clinton and Cornwallis, and a battery on Sullivan's Island, which terminated very fortunately for America. I will endeavour to enclose with this, a printed account of it. It has given us good spirits here, and will have a happy effect upon our armies at New York and Ticonderoga. Surely our northern soldiers will not suffer themselves to be outdone by their brethren so nearly under the sun. I don't yet hear of any Massachusetts men at New York. Our people must not flinch, at this critical moment, when their country is in more danger than it ever will be again, perhaps. What will they say, if the Howes should prevail against our forces, at so important a post as New

¹ Mrs. Adams had gone into Boston with her children, to be inoculated with the small pox.

York, for want of a few thousand men from the Massachusetts? I will likewise send you by this post, Lord Howe's letter and proclamation, which has let the cat out of the bag. These tricks deceive no longer. Gentlemen here, who either were or pretended to be deceived heretofore, now see or pretend to see through such artifices. I apprehend his Lordship is afraid of being attacked upon Staten Island, and is throwing out his barrels to amuse Leviathan, until his reinforcements shall arrive.

LETTER LXVIII.

Philadelphia, 20 July, 1776.

THIS has been a dull day to me. I waited the arrival of the post with much solicitude and impatience, but his arrival made me more solicitous still. "To be left at the Post Office," in your handwriting on the back of a few lines from the Doctor, was all that I could learn of you and my little folks. If you were too busy to write, I hoped that some kind hand would have been found to let me know something about you. Do my friends think that I have been a politician so long, as to have lost all feeling? Do they suppose I have forgotten my wife and children? Or are they so panic-struck with the loss of Canada, as to be afraid to correspond with me ?   Or have they forgotten that you have a husband, and your children a father ?   What have I done, or omitted to do, that I should be thus forgotten and neglected in the most tender and affecting scene of my life ?   Don't mistake me. I don't blame you. Your time and thoughts must have been wholly taken up with your own and your family's situation and necessities ; but twenty other persons might have informed me.

I suspect that you intended to have run slily through the small pox with the family, without letting me know it, and then have sent me an account that you were all well.   This might be a kind intention, and if the design had succeeded, would have made me very joyous.   But the secret is out, and I am left to conjecture.   But as the faculty have this distemper so much under command, I will flatter myself with the hope and expectation of soon hearing of your recovery.

LETTER LXIX.

Philadelphia, 29 July, 1776.

How are you all this morning ?   Sick, weak, faint, in pain, or pretty well recovered ?   By this time, you are well acquainted with the small pox. Pray, how do you like it ?

We have no news. It is very hard that half a dozen or half a score armies can't supply us with news. We have a famine, a perfect dearth of this necessary article. I am, at this present writing, perplexed and plagued with two knotty problems in politics. You love to pick a political bone. So I will even throw it to you.

If a confederation should take place, one great question is, how we shall vote. Whether each colony shall count one ? or whether each shall have a weight in proportion to its number, or wealth, or exports and imports, or a compound ratio of all ? Another is, whether Congress shall have authority to limit the dimensions of each colony, to prevent those, which claim by charter, or proclamation, or commission to the south sea, from growing too great and powerful, so as to be dangerous to the rest?

Shall I write you a sheet upon each of these questions ? When you are well enough to read, and I can find leisure enough to write, perhaps I may.

Gerry carried with him a canister for you. But he is an old bachelor, and what is worse, a politician, and what is worse still, a kind of soldier, so that I suppose he will have so much curiosity to see armies and fortifications, and assemblies, that you will lose many a fine breakfast at a time when you want them most.

Tell Betsey that this same Gerry is such another as herself, sex excepted. How is my brother and friend Cranch ? How is his other self and their little selves, and ours ? Don't be in the dumps, above all things. I am hard put to it to keep out of them, when I look at home. But I will be gay if I can.

Adieu.

LETTER LXX.

[Philadelphia], 3 August, 1776.

THE post was later than usual to-day, so that I had not yours of July 24, till this evening. You have made me very happy, by the particular and favorable account you give me, of all the family. But I don't understand how there are so many, who have no eruptions and no symptoms. The inflammation in the arm might do, but without these, there is no small pox. I will lay a wager, that your whole hospital has not had so much small pox as Mrs. Katy Quincy. Upon my word, she has had an abundance of it, but is finally recovered, looks as fresh as a rose, but pitted all over, as thick as ever you saw any one. I, this evening, presented your compliments, and thanks to Mr. Hancock, for his polite offer of his house, and likewise your compliments to his lady and Mrs. Katy.

4 August.

Went this morning to the Baptist meeting, in hopes of hearing Mr. Stillman, but was disappointed.. He was there, but another gentleman preached. His action was violent to a degree bordering on fury. His gestures unnatural and distorted. Not the least idea of grace in his motions, or elegance in his style. His voice was vociferous, and boisterous, and his composition almost wholly destitute of ingenuity. I wonder extremely at the fondness of our people for scholars educated at the southward, and for southern preachers. There is no one thing in which we excel them more, than in our university, our scholars and preachers. Particular gentlemen here, who have improved upon their education by travel, shine ; but in general, old Massachusetts outshines her younger sisters. Still in several particulars they have more wit than we. They have societies, the philosophical society particularly, which excites a scientific emulation, and propagates their fame. If ever I get through this scene of politics and war, I will spend the remainder of my days in endeavoring to instruct my countrymen, in the art of making the most of their abilities and virtues ; an art, which they have, hitherto, too much neglected. A philosophical society shall be established at Boston, if I have wit and address enough to accomplish it, sometime or other. Pray set brother Cranch's philosophical head to plodding upon this project. Many of his lucubrations would have been published and preserved, for the benefit of mankind, and for his honor, if such a club had existed.

My countrymen want art and address. They want knowledge of the world. They want the exterior and superficial accomplishment of gentlemen, upon which the world has set so high a value. In solid abilities and real virtues, they vastly excel, in general, any people upon this continent. Our New England people are awkward and bashful, yet they are pert, ostentatious and vain; a mixture, which excites ridicule and gives disgust. They have not the faculty of showing themselves to the best advantage, nor the art of concealing this faculty; an art and faculty which some people possess in the highest degree. Our deficiencies in these respects are owing wholly to the little intercourse we have with strangers, and to our inexperience in the world. These imperfections must be remedied, for New England must produce the heroes, the statesmen, the philosophers, or America will make no great figure, for some time.

Our army is rather sickly at New York, and we live in daily expectation of hearing of some great event. May God Almighty grant it may be prosperous for America. Hope is an anchor and a cordial. Disappointment, however, will not disconcert us.

If you will come to Philadelphia in September, I will stay as long as you please. I should be as proud and happy as a bridegroom.

Yours.

LETTER LXXI.

[Philadelphia], 12 August, 1776.

Mr. A.[1] sets off to-day, if the rain should not prevent him, with Colonel Whipple of Portsmouth, a brother of the celebrated Miss Hannah Whipple, a sensible and worthy man.   By him, I have sent you two bundles of letters, which I hope you will be careful of. I thought I should not be likely to find a safer opportunity.   By them, you will see, that my private correspondence alone is business enough for a lazy man. I think I have answered all but a few of those large bundles.

A French vessel, a pretty large brigantine, deeply laden, arrived here yesterday, from Martinique.   She had fifty barrels of limes, which are all sold, already, at such prices, that the amount of them will be sufficient to load the brig with flour.   A trade, we see, even now, in the midst of summer, is not totally interrupted by all the efforts of our enemies.   Prizes are taken, in no small numbers.   A gentleman told me a few days ago, that he had summed up the sugar, which has been taken, and it amounted to three thousand hogsheads, since which, two other ships have been taken, and carried into Maryland.   Thousands of schemes for privateering are afloat in American imaginations.

[1] Samuel Adams.

Some are for taking the Hull ships, with woollens, for Amsterdam and Rotterdam ; some are for the tin ships ; some for the Irish linen ships ; some, for outward bound, and others, for inward bound India-men ; some for the Hudson's bay ships, and many, for West India sugar ships. Out of these specula-tions, many fruitless and some profitable projects will grow.

We have no news from New York. All is quiet as yet. Our expectations are raised. The eyes of the world are upon Washington and Howe, and their armies. The wishes and prayers of the virtuous part of it, I hope, will be answered. If not, yet virtues grow out of affliction. I repeat my request that you would ask some of the members of the general court, if they can send me horses ; and if they cannot, that you would send them. I can live no longer without a servant and a horse.

LETTER LXXII.

[Philadelphia], 12 August, 1776.

Mr. A. and Colonel Whipple are at length gone. Colonel Tudor went off with them. They went away, about three o'clock this afternoon. I wrote by A. and Colonel Whipple too ; by the latter I sent two large bundles, which he promised to deliver to you. These middle States begin to taste the sweets of war. Ten thousand difficulties and wants occur, which they had no conception of before. Their militia are as clamorous, and impatient of discipline, and mutinous as ours, and more so. There has been seldom less than four thousand men in this city at a time, for a fortnight past, on their march to New Jersey. Here they wait, until we grow very angry about them, for canteens, camp kettles, blankets, tents, shoes, hose, arms, flints and other dittoes, while we are under a very critical solicitude for our army at New York, on account of the insufficiency of men.

I want to be informed of the state of things with you ; whether there is a scarcity of provisions of any kind, of West India articles, of clothing ? Whether any trade is carried on, any fishery ? Whether any vessels arrive from abroad, or whether any go to sea upon foreign voyages. I wish to know, likewise, what posture of defence you are in ? What fortifications are at Nantasket, at Long Island, Pettick's Island, &c., and what men and officers there are to garrison them ? We hear nothing from the Massachusetts, lately, in comparison of what we did, when the army was before Boston.

I must not conclude without repeating my request, that you would ask some of the members of the general court to send me horses, and if they cannot, to send them yourself.

LETTER LXXIII.

Philadelphia, 14 August, 1776.

THIS is the anniversary of a memorable day in the
history of America. A day when the principle of
American resistance and independence was first as-
serted and carried into action. The stamp office fell
before the rising spirit of our countrymen.[1] It is not
impossible that the two grateful brothers may make
their grand attack this very day. If they should, it is
possible it may be more glorious for this country, than
ever: it is certain, it will become more memorable.

Your favors of August 1st and 5th came by yesterday's post. I congratulate you all upon your agreeable prospects. Even my pathetic little hero Charles,
I hope, will have the distemper finely. It is very odd
that the Doctor cannot put infection enough into his
veins; nay, it is unaccountable to me, that he has not
taken it the natural way, before now. I am under
little apprehension, prepared as he is, if he should.
I am concerned about you, much more. So many
persons about you sick, the children troublesome, your
mind perplexed, yourself weak and relaxed. The
situation must be disagreeable. The country air and
exercise, however, will refresh you.

[1] Hutchinson, Vol. iii. p. 120.   Gordon, Vol. i. p. 175.

I am put upon a committee, to prepare a device for a golden medal, to commemorate the surrender of Boston to the American arms, and upon another, to prepare devices for a great seal, for the confederated States. There is a gentleman here of French extraction, whose name is Du Simitiere, a painter by profession, whose designs are very ingenious, and his drawings well executed. He has been applied to for his advice. I waited on him yesterday, and saw his sketches. For the medal he proposes, Liberty, with her spear and pileus, leaning on General Washington. The British fleet in Boston harbor with all their sterns towards the town, the American troops marching in. For the seal, he proposes, The arms of the several nations from whence America has been peopled, as English, Scotch, Irish, Dutch, German, &c., each in a shield. On one side of them, Liberty with her pileus, on the other, a rifler in his uniform, with his rifle gun in one hand, and his tomahawk in the other. This dress and these troops with this kind of armor being peculiar to America, unless the dress was known to the Romans. Dr. Franklin showed me yesterday a book, containing an account of the dresses of all the Roman soldiers, one of which appeared exactly like it. This M. du Simitiere is a very curious man. He has begun a collection of materials for a history of this revolution. He begins with the first advices of the tea ships. He cuts out of the newspapers every scrap of intelligence, and every piece of speculation, and pastes it upon clean paper, arranging them under the head of that State to which they belong, and intends to bind them up in volumes. He has a list of every speculation and pamphlet concerning independence, and another of those concerning forms of government.

Doctor F. proposes a device for a seal. Moses lifting up his wand, and dividing the red sea, and Pharaoh in his chariot overwhelmed with the waters. This motto. " Rebellion to tyrants is obedience to God."

Mr. Jefferson proposed, The children of Israel in the wilderness, led by a cloud by day, and a pillar of fire by night — and on the other side, Hengist and Horsa, the Saxon chiefs, from whom we claim the honor of being descended, and whose political principles and form of government we have assumed.

I proposed, The choice of Hercules, as engraved by Gribelin, in some editions of Lord Shaftesbury's works. The hero resting on his club. Virtue pointing to her rugged mountain on one hand, and persuading him to ascend. Sloth, glancing at her flowery paths of pleasure, wantonly reclining on the ground, displaying the charms both of her eloquence and person, to seduce him into vice. But this is too complicated a group for a seal or medal, and it is not original.

I shall conclude by repeating my request for horses and a servant. Let the horses be good ones. I can 't ride a bad horse so many hundred miles. If our affairs had not been in so critical a state at New York, I should have run away before now. But I am determined, now, to stay until some gentleman is sent here in my room, and until my horses come. But the time will be very tedious.

The whole force is arrived at Staten Island.

LETTER LXXIV.

Philadelphia, 18 August, 1776.

My letters to you are an odd mixture. They would appear to a stranger like the dish which is sometimes called omnium gatherum. This is the first time, I believe, that these two words were ever put together in writing. The literal interpretation I take to be " a collection of all things." But, as I said before, the words having never before been written, it is not possible to be very learned in telling you what the Arabic, Syriac, Chaldaic, Greek and Roman commentators say upon the subject. Amidst all the rubbish that constitutes the heap, you will see a proportion of affection for my friends, my family and country, that gives a complexion to the whole. I have a very tender, feeling heart. This country knows not, and never can know the torments, I have endured for its sake. I am glad it never can know, for it would give more pain to the benevolent and humane, than I could wish even the wicked and malicious to feel.

I have seen in this world but a little of that pure

flame of patriotism which certainly burns in some breasts. There is much of the ostentation and affectation of it. I have known a few, who could not bear to entertain a selfish design, nor to be suspected by others of such a meanness ; but these are not the most respected by the world. A man must be selfish, even to acquire great popularity. He must grasp for himself, under specious pretences for the public good, and he must attach himself to his relations, connexions, and friends, by becoming a champion for their interests, in order to form a phalanx about him for his own defence, to make them trumpeters of his praise, and sticklers for his fame, fortune and honor.

My friend Warren, the late Governor Ward, and Mr. Gadsden are three characters, in which I have seen the most generous disdain of every spice and species of such meanness. The two last had not great abilities, but they had pure hearts. Yet they had less influence than many others, who had neither so considerable parts, nor any share at all of their purity of intention. Warren has both talents and virtues beyond most men in this world, yet his character has never been in proportion. Thus it always is, and has been and will be. Nothing has ever given me more mortification than a suspicion that has been propagated of me, that I am actuated by private views, and have been aiming at high places. The office of chief justice has occasioned this jealousy, and it never will be allayed, until I resign it. Let me have my farm, family and goosequill, and all the honors and offices this world has to bestow, may go to those, who deserve them better and desire them more. I court them not.

There are very few people in this world with whom
I can bear to converse. I can treat all with decency
and civility, and converse with them, when it is necessary, on points of business. But I am never happy
in their company. This has made me a recluse, and
will, one day, make me a hermit. I had rather build
stone wall upon Penn's hill, than to be the first prince
in Europe, or the first General, or first Senator in
America.

Our expectations are very high of some great affair at New York.

———

LETTER LXXV.

Philadelphia, 21 August, 1776.

YESTERDAY morning, I took a walk into Arch street
to see Mr. Peale's Painter's room. Peale is from Maryland, a tender, soft, affectionate creature. He
showed me a large picture, containing a group of figures, which, upon inquiry, I found were his family ;
his mother and his wife's mother, himself and his wife,
his brothers and sisters, and his children, sons and
daughters, all young. There was a pleasant, a happy cheerfulness in their countenances, and a familiarity in their air towards each other.

He showed me one moving picture. His wife, all

bathed in tears, with a child about six months old, laid out upon her lap. This picture struck me prodigiously. He has a variety of portraits, very well done, but not so well as Copley's portraits. Copley is the greatest master that ever was in America. His portraits far exceed West's. Peale has taken General Washington, Dr. Franklin, Mrs. Washington, Mrs. Rush, Mrs. Hopkinson, Mr. Blair McClenachan and his little daughter in one picture, his lady and her little son in another. Peale showed me some books upon the art of painting. Among the rest one by Sir Joshua Reynolds, the President of the English Academy of painters, by whom the pictures of General Conway and Colonel Barré, in Faneuil Hall, were taken. He showed me too, a great number of miniature pictures. Among the rest, Mr. Hancock and his lady, Mr. Smith of South Carolina, whom you saw the other day in Boston, Mr. Custis, and many others.

He showed me, likewise, draughts, or rather sketches, of gentlemen's seats in Virginia, where he had been, Mr. Corbin's, Mr. Page's, General Washington's, &c. Also a variety of rough drawings made by great masters in Italy, which he keeps as models. He showed me several imitations of heads, which he had made in clay, as large as the life, with his hands only Among the rest, one of his own head and face, which was a great likeness. He is ingenious. He has vanity, loves finery, wears a sword, gold lace, speaks French, is capable of friendship, and strong family attachments, and natural affections.

At this shop, I met Mr. Francis Hopkinson, late a

Mandamus Counsellor of New Jersey, now a member
of the continental Congress, who, it seems, is a native
of Philadelphia, a son of a prothonotary of this county, who was a person much respected. The son was
liberally educated, and is a painter and a poet. I
have a curiosity to penetrate a little deeper into the
bosom of this curious gentleman, and may possibly
give you some more particulars concerning him. He
is one of your pretty, little, curious, ingenious men.
His head is not bigger than a large apple, less than
our friend Pemberton, or Doctor Simon Tufts. I
have not met with anything in natural history more
amusing and entertaining than his personal appearance — yet he is genteel and well bred and is very
social.

I wish I had leisure and tranquillity of mind to
amuse myself with those elegant and ingenious arts of
painting, sculpture, statuary, architecture and music.
But I have not. A taste in all of them is an agreeable accomplishment. Mr. Hopkinson has taken in
crayons with his own hand a picture of Miss Keys, a
famous New Jersey beauty. He talks of bringing it
to town, and in that case, I shall see it, I hope.

Philadelphia, 25 August, 1776.

THE day before yesterday and yesterday, we expected letters and papers by the post, but by some accident, or mismanagement of the riders, no post is arrived yet, which has been a great disappointment to me. I watch with longing eyes for the post, because you have been very good, of late, in writing by every one. I long to hear that Charles is in as fair a way through the distemper, as the rest of you.

Poor Barrell is violently ill, in the next chamber to mine, of an inflammatory fever. I hear every cough, sigh and groan. His fate hangs in a critical suspense. The least thing may turn the scale against him. Miss Quincy is here, very humanely employed in nursing him. This goodness does her honor. Mr. Paine has recovered of his illness, and, by present appearances, is in better health than before. I hope it will not be my fate to be sick here. Indeed, I am not much afraid of these acute disorders; mine are more chronical, nervous and slow. I must have a ride. I cannot make it do without it.

We are now approaching rapidly to the autumnal equinox, and no great blow has yet been struck, in the martial way, by our enemies, nor by us. If we should be blessed, this year, with a few storms, as happy as those which fell out last year in the beginning of

September, they will do much for us. The British
fleet, where they now lie, have not a harbor so con-
venient or safe as they had, last year. Another winter, will do much for us too. We shall have more
and better soldiers. We shall be better armed. We
shall have a greater force at sea. We shall have
more trade. Our artillery will be greatly increased,
our officers will have more experience, and our soldiers more discipline, our politicians more courage
and confidence, and our enemies less hope. Our
American commonwealths will be all completely
formed and organized, and every thing, I hope, will go
on with greater vigor.

After I had written thus far, the post came in and
brought me your favor of the 14th of August. Abby
by this time, I conclude, is well and Charles, I hope,
is broken out. Don't you recollect, upon this occasion, Doctor Byles's benediction to me, when I was inoculated ? As you will see the piquancy of it now,
more than ever you could before, I will tell the story.

After having been ten or eleven days inoculated, I
lay lolling on my bed in Major Cunningham's chamber under the tree of liberty, with half a dozen young
fellows as lazy as myself, all waiting and wishing for
symptoms and eruptions, all of a sudden appeared at
the chamber door, the reverend Doctor with his rosy
face, many-curled wig and pontifical air and gait. "I
have been thinking," says he, "that the clergy of this
town ought, upon this occasion, to adopt the benediction of the romish clergy, and, when we enter the
apartment of the sick, to say in the foreign pronuncia-

tion, ' *Pax tecum.*'" These words are spoken by
foreigners, as the Doctor pronounced them, *Pox take
'em.* One would think Sir Isaac Newton's discovery
of the system of gravitation did not require a deeper
reach of thought than this frivolous pun.

Your sentiments of the importance of education in
women are exactly agreeable to my own. Yet the
femmes savantes, are contemptible characters. So
is that of a pedant universally, how muchsoever of a
male he may be. In reading history, you will generally observe, when you light upon a great character,
whether a general, a statesman, or philosopher, some
female about him, either in the character of a mother,
wife or sister, who has knowledge and ambition above
the ordinary level of women, and that much of his
eminence is owing to her precepts, example or instigation, in some shape or other. Let me mention an
example or two. Sempronius Gracchus and Caius
Gracchus, two great, though unfortunate men, are said
to have been instigated to their great actions by their
mother, who, in order to stimulate their ambition, told
them, that she was known in Rome by the title of the
mother-in-law of Scipio, not the mother of the Grac-
chi. Thus she excited their emulation and put them
upon reviving the old project of an equal division of
the conquered lands, (a genuine republican measure,
though it had been too long neglected to be then practicable,) in order to make their names as illustrious as
Scipio's.

The great Duke who first excited the Portuguese
to revolt from the Spanish monarchy, was spurred on

to his great enterprise by a most artful and ambitious wife, and thus indeed you will find it, very generally.

———

LETTER LXXVII.

Philadelphia, 5 September, 1776.

MR. BASS arrived this day with the joyful news that you were all well. By this opportunity, I shall send you a canister of green tea by Mr. Hare. Before Mr. Gerry went away from hence, I asked Mrs. Yard to send a pound of green tea to you. She readily agreed. When I came home at night I was told Mr. G. was gone I asked Mrs. Y. if she had sent the canister? She said, yes, and that Mr. G. undertook to deliver it with a great deal of pleasure. From that time I flattered myself you would have the poor relief of a dish of good tea, under all your fatigues with the children, and under all the disagreeable circumstances attending the small pox ; and I never conceived a single doubt that you had received it, until Mr. Gerry's return. I asked him, accidentally, whether he delivered it and he said, " Yes, to Mr. Samuel Adams's lady." [1] I was astonished. He misunderstood

———

[1] This mistake in the delivery of the tea is frequently mentioned in the letters of this period, and appears to have caused much amusement to the parties.

Mrs. Yard entirely, for upon inquiry, she affirms she told him, it was for Mrs. J. A. I was so vexed at this, that I have ordered another canister, and Mr. Hare has been kind enough to undertake to deliver it. How the dispute will be settled, I don't know. You must send a card to Mrs. S. A., and let her know, that the canister was intended for you, and she may send it you, if she chooses, as it was charged to me. It is amazingly dear. Nothing less than forty shillings, lawful money, a pound.

I am rejoiced that my horses are come. I shall now be able to take a ride. But it is uncertain when I shall set off for home. I will not go at present. Affairs are too delicate and critical. The panic may seize[1] whom it will. It shall not seize me. I will stay here until the public countenance is better, or much worse. It must and will be better. I think it is not now bad. Lies by the million will be told you. Don't believe any of them. There is no danger of the communication being cut off between the northern and southern colonies. I can go home when I please, in spite of all the fleet and army of Great Britain.

---

[1] On account of the defeat on Long Island.

LETTER LXXVIII.

[Philadelphia], Friday, 6 September, 1776.

This day, I think, has been the most remarkable of all. Sullivan came here from Lord Howe, five days ago, with a message, that his lordship desired a half an hour's conversation with some of the members of Congress in their private capacities. We have spent three or four days in debating, whether we should take any notice of it. I have, to the utmost of my abilities, during the whole time, opposed our taking any notice of it. But, at last, it was determined by a majority, " that the Congress being the representatives of the free and independent States of America, it was improper to appoint any of their members to confer in their private characters with his lordship. But they would appoint a committee of their body, to wait on him, to know whether he had power to treat with Congress upon terms of peace, and to hear any propositions that his lordship may think proper to make."

When the committee came to be balloted for, Dr. Franklin and your humble servant were unanimously chosen. Colonel R. H. Lee and Mr. Rutledge had an equal number ; but, upon a second vote, Mr. Rutledge was chosen. I requested to be excused, but was desired to consider of it until to-morrow. My friends here advise me to go. All the stanch and intrepid are very earnest with me to go, and the timid and wavering, if any such there are, agree in the request. So I believe I shall undertake the journey. I doubt whether his lordship will see us, but the same committee will be directed to inquire into the state of the army at New York, so that there will be business enough, if his lordship makes none. It would fill this letter-book to give you all the arguments, for and against this measure, if I had liberty to attempt it. His lordship seems to have been playing off a number of Machiavelian manœuvres, in order to throw upon us the odium of continuing this war. Those who have been advocates for the appointment of this committee are for opposing manœuvre to manœuvre, and are confident that the consequence will be, that the odium will fall upon him. However this may be, my lesson is plain, to ask a few questions and take his answers.

I can think of but one reason for their putting me upon this embassy, and that is this. An idea has crept into many minds here, that his lordship is such another as Mr. Hutchinson, and they may possibly think that a man who has been accustomed to penetrate into the mazy windings of Hutchinson's heart, and the serpentine wiles of his head, may be tolerably qualified to converse with his lordship.

Sunday, 8 September.

Yesterday's post brought me yours of August 29. The report you mention " that I was poisoned upon

my return home, at New York," I suppose will be
thought to be a prophecy delivered by the oracle, in
mystic language, and meant, that I should be political-
ly or morally poisoned by Lord Howe. But the prophecy shall be false.

LETTER LXXIX.

Philadelphia, Saturday, 14 September, 1776.

YESTERDAY morning, I returned with Dr. Franklin and
Mr. Rutledge from Staten Island, where we met Lord
Howe, and had about three hours' conversation with
him. The result of this interview will do no disser-
vice to us. It is now plain that his lordship has no
power, but what is given him in the act of Parliament. His commission authorizes him to grant pardons upon submission, and to converse, confer, consult and advise with such persons as he may think
proper, upon American grievances, upon the instructions to Governors and the acts of Parliament, and if
any errors should be found to have crept in, his majesty and the ministry were willing they should be rec-
tified.

I found yours of 31st of August and 2d of September. I now congratulate you on your return home with
the children. I am sorry to find you anxious on account of idle reports. Don't regard them. I think our

friends are to blame to mention such silly stories. What good do they expect to do by it ?

My ride has been of service to me.   We were absent but four days.   It was an agreeable excursion. His lordship is about fifty years of age.   He is a well bred man, but his address is not so irresistible as it has been represented.   I could name you many Americans, in your own neighborhood, whose art, address and abilities are greatly superior.   His head is rather confused, I think.

When I shall return I can't say.   I expect now every day fresh hands from Watertown.

LETTER LXXX.

[Philadelphia], 22 September, 1776.

WE have at last agreed upon a plan for forming a regular army.   We have offered twenty dollars and a hundred acres of land to every man who will enlist during the war.   And a new set of articles of war are agreed on.   I will send you, if I can, a copy of these resolutions and regulations.

I am at a loss what to write.   News we have not. Congress seems to be forgotten by the armies.   We are most unfaithfully served in the post office, as well as many other offices, civil and military.   Unfaithfulness in public stations is deeply criminal.   But there

is no encouragement to be faithful. Neither profit,
nor honor, nor applause is acquired by faithfulness.
But I know by what.   There is too much corruption ·
even in this infant age of our republic.   Virtue is not
in fashion.   Vice is not infamous.

                                        1 October, 1776.

   Since I wrote the foregoing, I have not been able
to find time to write you a line. Although I cannot write you so often as I wish, you are never out of
my thoughts. I am repining at my hard lot in being
torn from you much oftener than I ought. I have
often mentioned to you the multiplicity of my engagements, and have been once exposed to the ridicule
and censure of the world for mentioning the great
importance of the business which lay upon me ; and
if this letter should ever see the light, it would be
again imputed to vanity that I mention to you how
busy I am. But I must repeat it by way of apology
for not writing you oftener. From four o'clock in the
morning until ten at night, I have not a single moment which I can call my own. I will not say, that I
expect to run distracted, to grow melancholy, to drop
in an apoplexy or fall into a consumption ; but I do
say, it is little less than a miracle, that one or other of
these misfortunes has not befallen me before now.
   Your favors of 15th, 20th, and 23d September, are
now before me. Every line from you gives me inexpressible pleasure, but it is a great grief to me that

can write no oftener to you. There is one thing which excites my utmost indignation and contempt. I mean the brutality with which people talk to you of my death. I beg you would openly affront every man, woman, or child, for the future, who mentions any such thing to you, except your relations and friends, whose affections you cannot doubt. I expect it of all my friends, that they resent, as affronts to me, every repetition of such reports.

I shall enclose to you Governor Livingston's speech. The most elegant and masterly ever made in America. Depend upon it, the enemy cannot cut off the communication. I can come home when I will. They have New York and this is their *ne plus ultra*.

LETTER LXXXI.

Philadelphia, 4 October, 1776.

I AM seated in a large library room with eight gentlemen round about me, all engaged in conversation. Amidst these interruptions, how shall I make it out to write a letter?

The first day of October, the day appointed by the charter of Pennsylvania for the annual election of Representatives, has passed away, and two counties only have chosen members, Bucks and Chester. The

Assembly is therefore dead and the convention is dissolved. A new convention is to be chosen the beginning of November. The proceedings of the late convention are not well liked by the best of the Whigs. Their constitution is reprobated, and the oath with which they have endeavored to prop it, by obliging every man to swear that he will not add to, or diminish from, or any way alter that constitution, before he can vote, is execrated.

We live in the age of political experiments. Among many that will fail, some I hope will succeed. But Pennsylvania will be divided and weakened, and rendered much less vigorous in the cause by the wretched ideas of government which prevail in the minds of many people in it.

LETTER LXXXII.

[Philadelphia], 8 October, 1776.

I ought to acknowledge with gratitude your constant kindness in writing to me by every post. Your favor of 29 September,[1] came by the last. I wish it had been in my power to have returned your civilities with the same punctuality, but it has not. Long before this, you have received letters from me, and newspa-

[1] Mrs. Adams's letters, Vol. I. p. 105.

pers containing a full account of the negotiation. The communication is still open, and the post-riders now do their duty, and will continue to do so.

I assure you, we are as much at a loss, about affairs at New York, as you are. In general, our Generals were outgeneraled on Long Island, and Sullivan and Stirling with a thousand men were made prisoners, in consequence of which and several other unfortunate circumstances, a council of war thought it prudent to retreat from that island and Governor's Island, and then from New York. They are now posted at Haerlem, about ten or eleven miles from the city. They left behind them some provisions, some cannon and some baggage. Wherever the men of war have approached, our militia have most manfully turned their backs and run away, officers and men, like sturdy fellows; and their panics have sometimes seized the regular regiments. One little skirmish on Montresor's Island ended with the loss of the brave Major Henley and the disgrace of the rest of the party. Another skirmish, which might indeed be called an action, ended in the defeat and shameful flight of the enemy with the loss of the brave Colonel Knowlton on our part. The enemy have possession of Paulus hook and Bergen point, places on the Jersey side of North river. By this time their force is so divided between Staten Island, Long Island, New York, Paulus hook, and Bergen point, that I think they will do no great matter more this fall, unless the expiration of the term of enlistment of our army should disband it. If our new enlistment fill up for soldiers during

the war, we shall do well enough.   Every body must
encourage this.

You are told that a regiment of Yorkers behaved
ill, and it may be true ; but I can tell you that several regiments of Massachusetts men behaved ill too.
The spirit of venality you mention is the most dreadful and alarming enemy America has to oppose.   It
is as rapacious and insatiable as the grave.   We are
in the *fæce Romuli non republica Platonis.*   This
predominant avarice will ruin America, if she is ever
ruined.   If God Almighty does not interpose by his
grace to control this universal idolatry to the mammon
of unrighteousness we shall be given up to the chas-
tisements of his judgments.   I am ashamed of the age
I live in.

You surprise me with your account of the prayers
in public for an abdicated King, a pretender to the
crown.   Nothing of that kind is heard in this place,
or any other part of the continent, but New York and
the place you mention.   This practice is treason
against the State, and cannot be long tolerated.

Don't leave off writing to me.   I write as often as
I can.   I am glad master John has an office so useful
to his mamma and papa as that of post-rider.

LETTER LXXXIII.

Philadelphia, 11 October, 1776.

I SUPPOSE your ladyship has been in the twitters for some time, because you have not received a letter by every post, as you used to do. But I am coming to make my apology in person. I yesterday, asked and obtained leave of absence. It will take me till next Monday to get ready, to finish off a few remnants of public business, and to put my private affairs in proper order. On the 14th day of October I shall get away, perhaps. But I don't expect to reach home in less than a fortnight, perhaps not in three weeks, as I shall be obliged to make stops by the way.

LETTER LXXXIV.

Dedham, 9 January, 1777.

MY DEAR,

THE irresistible hospitality of Dr. Sprague and his lady has prevailed upon me and my worthy fellow

---

¹ During the interval, marked by the dates of this and the preceding letter, Mr. Adams was at home. He was now returning to Congress.

traveller to put up at his happy seat. We had an agreeable ride to this place, and to-morrow morning, we set off for Providence, or some other route.

Present my affection in the tenderest manner to my little deserving daughter and my amiable sons. It was cruel parting this morning. My heart was most deeply affected although I had the presence of mind to appear composed. May God Almighty's providence protect you, my dear, and all our little ones. My good genius, my guardian angel, whispers me, that we shall see happier days, and that I shall live to enjoy the felicities of domestic life with her, whom my heart esteems above all earthly blessings.

LETTER LXXXV.

Hartford, 13 January, 1777.

THE riding has been so hard and rough, and the weather so cold, that we have not been able to push further than this place. My little colt has performed very well hitherto, and I think, will carry me through this journey very pleasantly.

Our spirits have been cheered by two or three pieces of good news, which Commissary Trumbull, who is now with me, tells us he saw yesterday, in a letter from General Washington, who has gained another considerable advantage of the enemy at Stony Brook, in the Jerseys, as General Putnam has gained another at Burlington, and the Jersey militia a third. The particulars you will have, before this reaches you, in the public prints. The communication of intelligence begins to be more open, and we have no apprehensions of danger in the route we shall take. Howe has reason to repent of his rashness, and will have more.

My love to my dear little ones. They are all very good children, and I have no doubt will continue so. I will drop a line as often as I can.

Adieu.

LETTER LXXXVI.

Hartford, 14 January, 1777.

It is now generally believed that General Washington has killed and taken at least two thousand of Mr. Howe's army since Christmas. Indeed the evidence of it is from the General's own letters. You know I ever thought Mr. Howe's march through the Jerseys a rash step. It has proved so. But how much more so would it have been thought, if the Americans could all have viewed it in that light, and exerted themselves, as they might and ought. The whole flock would infallibly have been taken in the net.

The little nest of hornets in Rhode Island ! Is it to remain unmolested this winter ? The honor of New England is concerned. If they are not ousted, I will never again glory in being a New England man. There are now New England Generals, officers and soldiers, and if something is not done, any man may, after that, call New England men poltroons, with all my heart.

LETTER LXXXVII.

Fishkill, 1777.

AFTER a march like that of Hannibal over the Alps, we arrived, last night, at this place, where we found the utmost difficulty to get forage for our horses, and lodgings for ourselves, and, at last, were indebted to the hospitality of a private gentleman, Colonel Brink-hoff, who very kindly cared for us.

We came from Hartford through Farmington, Southington, Waterbury, Woodbury, New Milford, New Fairfield, the oblong, &c. to Fishkill. Of all the mountains I ever passed, these are the worst. We found one advantage, however, in the cheapness of travelling. I don't find one half of the discontent, nor of the terror, here, that I left in the Massachusetts. People seem sanguine that they shall do something grand this winter.

I am well and in good spirits. My horse performs

extremely well.   He clambers over mountains that my old mare would have stumbled on.   The weather has been dreadfully severe.

LETTER LXXXVIII.

Poughkeepsie, 19 January, 1777.

THERE is too much ice in Hudson's river to cross it in ferry boats, and too little to cross it without, in most places, which has given us the trouble of riding up the Albany road, as far as this place, where we expect to go over on the ice, but if we should be disappointed here, we must go up as far as Esopus, about fifteen miles further.

This, as well as Fishkill, is a pretty village.   We are almost wholly among the Dutch.   Zealous against the Tories, who have not half the tranquillity here, that they have in the town of Boston, after all the noise that has been made about New York Tories. We are treated with the utmost respect, wherever we go, and have met with nothing like an insult from any person whatever.   I heard ten reflections, and twenty sighs and groans, among my constituents, to one here.

I shall never have done hoping that my countrymen will contrive some *coup de main* for the wretches at Newport.   The winter is the time.   Our enemies have divided their force.   Let us take advantage of it.

LETTER LXXXIX.

Bethlehem, Orange County,
State of New York, 20 January, 1777.

This morning, we crossed the North River, at Pough-keepsie, on the ice, after having ridden many miles on the east side of it, to find a proper place. We landed at New Marlborough, and passed through that and Newborough, to New Windsor, where we dined. This place is nearly opposite to Fishkill, and but little above the Highlands, where Fort Constitution and Fort Montgomery stand. The Highlands are a grand sight, a range of vast mountains which seem to be rolling like a tumbling sea. From New Windsor we came to this place, where we put up, and now we have a free and uninterrupted passage in a good road to Pennsylvania.

General Washington, with his little army, is at Morristown. Cornwallis, with his larger one, at Bruns-wick. Oh! that the continental army was full. Now is the time!

My little horse holds out finely, although we have lost much time, and travelled a great deal of un-necessary way, to get over the North River. We have reports of our people's taking Fort Washington again, and taking four hundred more prisoners, and six more pieces of cannon. But as I know not the persons who bring these accounts, I pay no attention to them.

LETTER XC.

Easton, at the Forks of Delaware river, in the
State of Pennsylvania, 24 January, 1777.

WE have at last crossed the Delaware and are agreeably lodged at Easton, a little town situated on a point
of land formed by the Delaware on one side, and the
river Lehigh on the other.   There is an elegant stone
church here, built by the Dutch people, by whom the
town is chiefly inhabited, and what is remarkable because uncommon, the Lutherans and Calvinists united
to build this church, and the Lutheran and Calvinist
ministers, alternately, officiate in it.   There is also a
handsome Court House.   The buildings, public and
private, are all of limestone.   Here are some Dutch
Jews.

Yesterday, we had the pleasure of seeing the Mo-
ravian mills in New Jersey.   These mills belong to
the society of Moravians in Bethlehem in Pennsylva
nia.   They are a great curiosity.   The building is of
limestone, four stories high.   It is not in my power
to give a particular description of this piece of me-
chanism.   A vast quantity of grain of all sorts is collected here.

We have passed through the famous county of
Sussex in New Jersey, where the Sussex Court House
stands, and where, we have so often been told, the
Tories are so numerous and dangerous.   We met

with no molestation nor insult. We stopped at some of the most noted Tory houses, and were treated every where with the utmost respect. Upon the strictest inquiry I could make, I was assured, that a great majority of the inhabitants are stanch whigs. Sussex, they say, can take care of Sussex. And yet all agree that there are more Tories in that county than in any other. If the British army should get into that county, in sufficient numbers to protect the Tories, there is no doubt to be made, they would be insolent enough, and malicious and revengeful. But there is no danger, at present, and will be none, until that event takes place. The weather has been sometimes bitterly cold, sometimes warm, sometimes rainy, and sometimes snowy, and the roads abominably hard and rough, so that this journey has been the most tedious I ever attempted. Our accommodations have been often very bad, but much better and cheaper than they would have been, if we had taken the road from Peekskill to Morristown, where the army lies.

LETTER XCI.

Baltimore, 2 February, 1777.

LAST evening, we arrived safe in this town, after the longest journey and through the worst roads and the

worst weather that I have ever experienced. My horses performed extremely well.

Baltimore is a very pretty town, situated on Patapsco river, which empties itself into the great bay
of Chesapeake. The inhabitants are all good Whigs,
having some time ago banished all the Tories from
among them. The streets are very dirty and miry,
but every thing else is agreeable, except the monstrous prices of things. We cannot get a horse kept
under a guinea a week. Our friends are well.

The continental army is filling up fast, here and
in Virginia. I pray that the Massachusetts may not
fail of its quota in season. In this journey we have
crossed four mighty rivers ; Connecticut, Hudson,
Delaware and Susquehannah. The two first, we
crossed upon the ice, the two last, in boats ; the last,
we crossed a little above the place where it empties
into Chesapeake Bay.

I think I have never been better pleased with any
of our American States than with Maryland. We
saw most excellent farms all along the road, and what
was more striking to me, I saw more sheep and flax
in Maryland than I ever saw in riding a like distance
in any other State. We scarce passed a farm without seeing a fine flock of sheep, and scarce a house
without seeing men or women dressing flax. Several
times we saw women breaking and swingling this
necessary article.

I have been to meeting and heard my old acquaint-
ance, Mr. Allison, a worthy clergyman of this town,
whom I have often seen in Philadelphia.

LETTER XCII.

Baltimore, 3 February, 1777.

THIS day has been observed in this place with exemplary decency and solemnity, in consequence of an
appointment of the government, in observance of a
recommendation of Congress, as a day of fasting. I
went to the Presbyterian meeting, and heard Mr. Allison deliver a most pathetic and animating as well as
pious, patriotic, and elegant discourse. I have seldom
been better pleased or more affected with a sermon.
The Presbyterian meeting house in Baltimore, stands
upon a hill just at the back of the town, from whence
we have a very fair prospect of the town and of the
water upon which it stands, and of the country round
it. Behind this eminence, which is the Beacon Hill
of Baltimore, lies a beautiful meadow, which is entirely encircled by a stream of water. This most
beautiful scene must be partly natural and partly artificial. Beyond the meadow and canal, you have a
charming view of the country. Besides the meeting
house, there is, upon this height, a large and elegant
Court House, as yet unfinished within, and a small
church of England, in which an old clergyman offici-
ates, Mr. Chase, father of Mr. Chase one of the delegates of Maryland, who, they say, is not so zealous a
Whig as his son.

I shall take opportunities to describe this town and

State more particularly to you hereafter. I shall inquire into their religion, their laws, their customs,
their manners, their descent and education, their
learning, their schools and colleges, and their morals.
It was said of Ulysses, I think, that he saw the manners of many men and many cities, which is like to
be my case, as far as American men and cities ex-
tend, provided Congress should continue in the rolling
humor, which I hope they will not. I wish however
that my mind was more at rest than it is, that I might
be able to make more exact observation of men and
things, as far as I go.

When I reflect upon the prospect before me, of so
long an absence from all that I hold dear in this world,
I mean, all that contributes to my private personal
happiness, it makes me melancholy. God Almighty's providence protect and bless you, and yours and
mine.

———

LETTER XCIII.

Baltimore, 7 February, 1777.

I AM at last, after a great deal of difficulty, settled in
comfortable quarters, but at an infinite expense. The
price I pay for my board is more moderate than any
other gentlemen give, excepting my colleagues, who

are all in the same quarters and at the same rates, except Mr. Hancock, who keeps a house by himself. The prices of things here are much more intolerable than at Boston. The attempt of New England to regulate prices is extremely popular in Congress, who will recommend an imitation of it to the other States. For my own part I expect only a partial and a temporary relief from it, and I fear that, after a time, the evils will break out with greater violence. The water will flow with greater rapidity for having been dammed up for a time. The only radical cure will be to stop the emission of more paper, and to draw in some that is already out, and devise means effectually to support the credit of the rest. To this end we must begin forthwith to tax the people as largely as the distressed circumstances of the country will bear. We must raise the interest from four to six per cent. We must, if possible, borrow silver and gold from abroad. We must, above all things, endeavor, this winter, to gain further advantages of the enemy, that our power may be in somewhat higher reputation than it is, or rather, than it has been.

LETTER XCIV.

Baltimore, 7 February, 1777.

I THINK, in some letter I sent you since I left Bethlehem, I promised you a more particular account of that curious and remarkable town. When we first came in sight of the town we found a country better cultivated and more agreeably diversified with prospects of orchards and fields, groves and meadows, hills and valleys, than any we had seen. When we came into the town, we were directed to a public house, kept by a Mr. Johnson, which, I think, was the best inn I ever saw. It belongs, it seems, to the society, is furnished at their expense, and is kept for their profit or at their loss. Here you might find every accommodation that you could wish for yourself, your servants and horses, and at no extravagant rates neither.

The town is regularly laid out, the streets straight and at right angles, like those in Philadelphia. It stands upon an eminence, and has a fine large brook flowing on one end of it, and the Lehigh, a branch of the Delaware, on the other. Between the town and the Lehigh are beautiful public gardens. They have carried the mechanical arts to greater perfection here than in any place which I have seen. They have a set of pumps which go by water, which force the water up through leaden pipes from the river to the top of the hill, near a hundred feet, and to the top of a little building in the shape of a pyramid or obelisk, which stands upon the top of the hill, and is twenty or thirty feet high. From this fountain, water is conveyed in pipes to every part of the town. Upon the river they have a fine set of mills. The best grist mills and bolting mills that are any where to be found. The best fulling mills, an oil mill, a mill to grind bark for the tanyard, a dying house where all colors are died, machines for shearing cloth, &c.

There are three public institutions here of a very remarkable nature. One, a society of the young men, another of the young women, and a third of the widows. There is a large building divided into many apartments, where the young men reside by themselves and carry on their several trades. They pay a rent to the society for their rooms and they pay for their board and what they earn is their own. There is another large building appropriated in the same manner to the young women. There is a governess a little like the lady abbess in some other institutions, who has the superintendence of the whole, and they have elders. Each apartment has a number of young women who are vastly industrious, some spinning, some weaving, others employed in all the most curious works in linen, wool, cotton, silver and gold, silk and velvet. This institution displeased me much. Their dress was uniform and clean, but very inelegant. Their rooms were kept extremely warm with Dutch stoves : and the heat, the want of fresh air and exercise relaxed the poor girls in such a manner as must, I think, destroy their health. Their countenances were languid and pale.

The society of widows is very similar. Industry and economy are remarkable in all these institutions. They showed us their church, which is hung with pictures of our Saviour, from his birth to his death, resurrection and ascension. It is done with very strong colors and very violent passions, but not in a very elegant taste. The painter, who is still living in Bethlehem, but very old, has formerly been in Italy, the school of painting. They have a very good organ in their church, of their own make. They have a public building on purpose for the reception of the dead, to which the corpse is carried as soon as it expires, where it lies until the time of sepulture.

Christian love is their professed object, but it is said they love money and make their public institutions subservient to the gratification of that passion. They suffer no lawsuits with one another, and as few as possible with other men. It is said that they now profess to be against war. They have a custom peculiar respecting courtship and marriage. The elders pick out pairs to be coupled together, who have no opportunity of conversing together, more than once or twice, before the knot is tied. The youth of the two sexes have very little conversation with one another before marriage.

Mr. Hassey, a very agreeable, sensible gentleman, who showed us the curiosities of the place, told me, upon inquiry, that they profess the Augsburg confession of faith, are Lutherans rather than Calvinists, distinguish between bishops and presbyters, but have no idea of the necessity of the uninterrupted succession, are very liberal and candid in their notions in opposition to bigotry, and live in charity with all denominations.

LETTER XCV.

Baltimore, 10 February, 1777.

FELL's point, which I mentioned in a letter this morning, has a considerable number of houses upon it.
The shipping all lies now at this point. You have
from it on one side a complete view of the harbor,
and on the other a fine prospect of the town of Baltimore. You see the hill in full view and the court
house, the church and meeting house upon it. The
court house makes a haughty appearance from this
point. There is a fortification erected on this point,
with a number of embrasures for cannon facing the
Narrows which make the entrance into the harbor.
At the Narrows they have a fort with a garrison in it.

It is now a month and a few days since I left you.
I have heard nothing from you nor received a letter
from the Massachusetts. I hope the post office will
perform better than it has done. I am anxious to
hear how you do. My duty to your papa and my
mother. Love to brothers and sisters. Tell Betsey
I hope she is married, though I want to throw the
stocking. My respects to Mr. Shaw. Tell him he may
be a Calvinist if he will, provided always, that he pre-
serves his candor, charity and moderation. What
shall I say of or to my children? What will they say
to me for leaving them, their education and fortune
so much to the disposal of chance? May Almighty
and all gracious providence protect and bless them!

I have this day sent my resignation of a certain mighty office.[1] It has relieved me from a burden which has a long time oppressed me. But I am determined that while I am ruining my constitution of mind and body, and running daily risks of my life and fortune in defence of the independence of my country, I will not knowingly resign my own.

———

LETTER XCVI.

Baltimore, 15 February, 1777.

MR. HALL, by whom this letter will be sent, will carry several letters to you, which have been written and delivered to him several days. He has settled his business agreeably. I have not received a line from the Massachusetts since I left it. Whether we shall return to Philadelphia soon or not, I cannot say. I rather conjecture it will not be long. You may write to me, in Congress, and the letter will be brought me wherever I shall be.

I am settled now, agreeably enough, in my lodgings. There is nothing in this respect that lies uneasily upon my mind, except the most extravagant price which I am obliged to give for every thing. My con-

---

[1] The office of Chief Justice of Massachusetts.

stituents will think me extravagant, but I am not. I
wish I could sell or send home my horses, but I cannot. I must have horses and a servant, for Congress
will be likely to remove, several times, in the course
of the ensuing year. I am impatient to hear from
you, and most tenderly anxious for your health and
happiness. I am also most affectionately solicitous
for my dear children, to whom remember

Yours.[1]

We long to hear of the formation of a new army.
We shall lose the most happy opportunity of destroying the enemy this spring if we do not exert ourselves
instantly. We have from New Hampshire a Colonel
Thornton, a physician by profession, a man of humor.
He has a large budget of droll stories with which he
entertains company perpetually. I heard, about twenty
or five and twenty years ago, a story of a physician
in Londonderry, who accidentally met with one of our
New England enthusiasts, called exhorters. The fa-
natic soon began to examine the Doctor concerning
the articles of his faith and what he thought of original sin. " Why," says the Doctor, " I satisfy myself
about it in this manner. Either original sin is divisible or indivisible. If it is divisible, every descend-
ant of Adam and Eve must have a part and the share
which falls to each individual at this day is so small a
particle that I think it is not worth considering. If

---

[1] This letter appears to have been finished and then re-
sumed.

indivisible, then the whole quantity must have descended in a right line, and must now be possessed by one person only ; and the chances are millions and millions and millions to one, that that person is now in Asia or Africa, and that I have nothing to do with it." I told Thornton the story, and that I suspected him to be the man. He said he was. He belongs to Londonderry.

————

LETTER XCVII.

Baltimore, 17 February, 1777.

It was this day determined to adjourn, to-morrow week, to Philadelphia.

Howe, as you know my opinion always was, will repent his mad march through the Jerseys. The people of that Commonwealth begin to raise their spirits exceedingly and to be firmer than ever. They are actuated by resentment now, and resentment, coinciding with principle, is a very powerful motive.

I have got into the old routine of war office and Congress, which takes up my time in such a manner that I can scarce write a line. I have not time to think nor to speak. There is a United States Lottery abroad. I believe you had better buy a ticket and make a present of it to our four sweet ones. Let us try their luck. I hope they will be more lucky than their papa has ever been, or ever will be. I am as well as can be expected. How it happens I don't know, nor how long it will last. My disposition was naturally gay and cheerful, but the prospects I have ever had before me and these cruel times will make me melancholy. I, who would not hurt the hair of the head of any animal, I, who am always made miserable by the misery of every susceptible being that comes to my knowledge, am obliged to hear continual accounts of the barbarities, the cruel murders in cold blood even by the most tormenting ways of starving and freezing, committed by our enemies, and continued accounts of the deaths and diseases contracted by their own imprudence. These accounts harrow me beyond description. These incarnate demons say in great composure, that " humanity is a yankee virtue, but that they are governed by policy." Is there any policy on this side of hell, that is inconsistent with humanity ? I have no idea of it. I know of no policy, God is my witness, but this, piety, humanity and honesty are the best policy. Blasphemy, cruelty and villany have prevailed and may again. But they won't prevail against America in this contest, because 1 find, the more of them are employed, the less they succeed.

Baltimore, 21 February, 1777.

YESTERDAY I had the pleasure of dining with Mr.
Purviance. There are two gentlemen of this name in
Baltimore, Samuel and Robert, eminent merchants
and in partnership. We had a brilliant company, the
two Mrs. Purviances, the two Lees, the ladies of the
two Colonels R. H. and F., Mrs. Hancock and Miss
Katy, and a young lady that belongs to the family.
If this letter, like some other wise ones, should be intercepted, I suppose I shall be called to account for
not adjusting the rank of these ladies a little better.
Mr. Hancock, the two Colonel Lees, Colonel Whipple,
Colonel Page, Colonel Ewing, the two Mr. Purviances
and a young gentleman. I fancy I have named all the
company. How happy would this entertainment
have been to me if I could, by a single volition, have
transported one lady about five hundred miles. But
alas! this is a greater felicity than falls to my share.
We have voted to go to Philadelphia next week.

We have made General Lincoln a continental Major General. We shall make Colonel Glover a Brigadier. I sincerely wish we could hear more from General Heath. Many persons are extremely dissatisfied
with numbers of the general officers of the highest
rank. I don't mean the Commander-in-chief, his
character is justly very high, but Schuyler, Putnam,
Spencer, Heath, are thought by very few to be

capable of the great commands they hold. We hear of none of their heroic deeds of arms. I wish they would all resign. For my part I will vote upon the genuine principles of a republic for a new election of general officers annually, and every man shall have my consent to be left out, who does not give sufficient proof of his qualifications.

I wish my lads were old enough. I would send every one of them into the army in some capacity or other. Military abilities and experience are a great advantage to any character.

LETTER XCIX.

Philadelphia, 7 March, 1777.

THE President, who is just arrived from Baltimore, came in, a few minutes ago, and delivered me yours of February 8, which he found at Susquehannah river, on its way to Baltimore. It gives me great pleasure to find that you have received so many letters from me, although I knew they contained nothing of importance. I feel a restraint in writing, like that which you complain of, and am determined to go on trifling. However, the post now comes regularly, and I believe you may trust it. I am anxious and impatient to hear of the march of the Massachusetts soldiers for the new army. They are much wanted.

This city is a dull place, in comparison of what it was. More than one half of the inhabitants have removed into the country, as it was their wisdom to do. The remainder are chiefly Quakers, as dull as beetles. From these neither good is to be expected nor evil to be apprehended. They are a kind of neutral tribe, or the race of the insipids. Howe may possibly attempt this town, and a pack of sordid scoundrels, male and female, seem to have prepared their minds and bodies, houses and cellars for his reception; but these are few, and more despicable in character than number. America will lose nothing by Howe's gaining this town. No such panic will be spread by it now, as was spread by the expectation of it in December. However, if we can get together twenty thousand men by the first of April, Mr. Howe will scarcely cross Delaware river this year. New Jersey may yet be his tomb, where he will have a monument very different from his brother's[1] in Westminster Abbey.

I am very uneasy that no attempt is made at Rhode Island. There is but a handful left there, who might be made an easy prey. The few invalids, who are left there, are scattered over the whole island, which is eleven miles in length, and three or four wide. Are New England men such sons of sloth and fear, as to lose this opportunity ? We may possibly remove again from hence, perhaps to Lancaster or Reading. It is good to change place ; it promotes health and

---

[1] Erected at the expense of Massachusetts Bay, pursuant to a vote of the General Court in 1758. See Hutchinson's History, Vol. iii. p. 71.

spirits; it does good many ways; it does good to the place we remove from, as well as to that we remove to, and it does good to those who move. I long to be at home, at the opening spring, but this is not my felicity. I am tenderly anxious for your health and for the welfare of the whole house.

LETTER C.

Philadelphia, 16 March, 1777.

THE spring advances very rapidly, and all nature will soon be clothed in her gayest robes. The green grass which begins to show itself here and there, revives in my longing imagination my little farm and its dear inhabitants. What pleasure has not this vile war deprived me of? I want to wander in my meadows, to ramble over my mountains, and to sit, in solitude, or with her who has all my heart, by the side of the brooks. These beautiful scenes would contribute more to my happiness than the sublime ones which surround me. I begin to suspect that I have not much of the grand in my composition. The pride and pomp of war, the continual sound of drums and fifes as well played as any in the world, the prancings and tramplings of the Light Horse, numbers of whom are paraded in the streets every day, have no charms for me. I long for rural and domestic scenes, for the warbling of birds, and prattle

of my children. Don't you think I am somewhat
poetical this morning for one of my years, and considering the gravity and insipidity of my employment ?   As much as I converse with sages and heroes,
they have very little of my love or admiration. I
should prefer the delights of a garden to the dominion
of a world. I have nothing of Cæsar's greatness in
my soul. Power has not my wishes in her train.
The Gods, by granting me health and peace and
competence, the society of my family and friends,
the perusal of my books and the enjoyment of my
farm and garden, would make me as happy as my
nature and state will bear. Of that ambition which
has power for its object, I don't believe I have a
spark in my heart. There are other kinds of ambition of which I have a great deal.[1]

I am now situated in a pleasant part of the town,
in Walnut street, on the south side of it, between
Second and Third streets, at the house of Mr. Duncan, a
gentleman from Boston, who has a wife and three
children.   General Wolcott, of Connecticut, and
Colonel Whipple, of Portsmouth, are with me in the
same house.   Mr. Adams has removed to Mrs.
Cheesman's, in Fourth street, near the corner of Market street, where he has a curious group of company,
consisting of characters as opposite as north and
south. Ingersoll, the stamp man and Judge of Ad-

---

[1] This letter is taken from the copy book, in which is
added, at this place, the following : " Note, 9 April. Literary
and professional, I suppose. But is not the heart deceitful
above all things ? "

miralty; Sherman, an old puritan, as honest as an angel and as firm in the cause of American independence as mount Atlas; and Colonel Thornton, as droll and funny as Tristram Shandy. Between the fun of Thornton, the gravity of Sherman, and the formal toryism of Ingersoll, Adams will have a curious life of it. The landlady, too, who has buried four husbands, one tailor, two shoemakers and Gilbert Tenant, and still is ready for a fifth, and well deserves him too, will add to the entertainment. Gerry and Lovell are yet at Miss Leonard's, under the auspices of Mrs. Yard. Mr. Hancock has taken a house in Chestnut street, near the corner of Fourth street, near the State House.

17 March.

We this day received letters from Dr. Franklin and Mr. Deane. I am not at liberty to mention particulars, but in general, the intelligence is very agreeable. I am now convinced there will be a general war.

LETTER CI.

Philadelphia, 28 March, 1777.

" A PLOT, a plot! a horrid plot! Mr. A.," says my barber, this morning. " It must be a plot, first, because there is British gold in it; second, because there is a woman in it; third, because there is a Jew in it; fourth, because I don't know what to make of it."

The barber means that a villain was taken up and examined yesterday, who appears, by his own confession, to have been employed, by Lord Howe and Jo. Galloway, to procure pilots to conduct the fleet up Delaware river and through the Chevaux de Frise. His confidant was a woman, who is said to be kept by a Jew. The fellow and the woman will suffer for their wickedness.

LETTER CII.

Philadelphia, 31 March, 1777.

I KNOW not the time when I have omitted to write you so long. I have received but three letters from you since we parted, and these were short ones. Do you write by the post? If you do, there must be some legerdemain. The post comes now constantly, once a week, and brings me newspapers, but no letters. I have ventured to write by the post, but whether my letters are received or not, I don't know. If you distrust the post, the speaker or your uncle Smith will find frequent opportunities of conveying letters.

I never was more desirous of hearing from home, and never before heard so seldom. We have reports here, not very favorable to the town of Boston. It is said that dissipation prevails, and that toryism abounds, and is openly avowed at the coffee-houses. I hope the reports are false. Apostasies in Boston are more abominable than in any other place. Toryism finds worse quarter here. A poor fellow detected here as a spy, employed, as he confesses by Lord Howe and Mr. Galloway, to procure pilots for Delaware river and for other purposes, was this day at noon executed on the gallows, in the presence of an immense crowd of spectators. His name was James Molesworth. He has been Mayor's Clerk to three or four Mayors.

I believe you will think my letters very trifling — indeed they are. I write in trammels. Accidents have thrown so many letters into the hands of the enemy, and they take such a malicious pleasure in exposing them, that I choose they should have nothing but trifles from me to expose. For this reason I never write any thing of consequence from Europe, from Philadelphia, from camp, or any where else. If I could write freely, I would lay open to you the whole system of politics and war, and would de-lineate all the characters in either drama, as minutely, although I could not do it so elegantly, as Tully did in his letters to Atticus.

We have letters however from France by a vessel in at Portsmouth.[1] Of her important cargo, you

[1] The ship *Mercury*, from Nantes, with military stores pro-cured by Mr. Deane, in France. *Journals of Congress*, Vol. iii. p. 106.

have heard. There is news of very great importance in the letters, but I am not at liberty. The news, however, is very agreeable.

———

LETTER CIII.[1]

[Philadelphia], 2 April, 1777.

YESTERDAY'S post brought me your kind favor of March 8th, 9th, 10th, with a letter enclosed from each of my sons ; but where is my daughter's letter ? That is missing. I regret the loss of it much. You think I dont't write politics enough. Indeed I have a sur-feit of them. But I shall give you now and then a taste, since you have such a gout for them.

By a letter of 17th January, Dr. Franklin, Mr. Deane, and Dr. Lee met in Paris, and on the 28th Decem-ber, had an audience of the Count de Vergennes, Sec-retary of state and minister of foreign affairs ; laid before him their commission with the articles of the proposed treaty of commerce ; were assured of the protection of his court, and that due consideration should be given to what they offered. Soon after, they

[1] This letter is a summary of the intelligence furnished in the first communication made to the Congress by the joint Commissioners at Paris. *Diplomatic Correspondence of the American Revolution*, Vol. i. p. 250.

presented a memorial on the situation of our States, drawn up at the minister's request, together with the articles of general confederation, and the demand for ships of war, agreeably to their instructions, copies of all which papers they gave to the Count d'Aranda, the Spanish ambassador, to be communicated to his Court. They were promised an answer from the French Court, as soon as they could know the determination of Spain, with whom they design to act with perfect unanimity. In the mean time, they are expediting several vessels laden with artillery, arms, ammunition and clothing.

The ports of France, Spain and Florence, (that is Leghorn in the Mediterranean) are open to the American cruisers upon the usual terms of neutrality. They write for commissions to be given to privateers, and for more frequent and authentic intelligence. Great efforts are now making by the British ministry to procure more troops from Germany. The princes in alliance with France have refused to lend any or to enter into any guarantee of Hanover, which England has been mean enough to ask, being apprehensive for that electorate, if she should draw from it any more of its troops. Four more regiments (two of them to be light horse,) are raising in Hesse, where there has been an insurrection on account of drafting the people, and now great sums of money are distributed for procuring men. They talk of ten thousand men in all, to be sent over this spring.

The hearts of the French are universally for us, and the cry is strong for immediate war with Britain.

Indeed, every thing tends that way, but the Count has reasons for postponing it a little longer. In the mean time preparations are making. They have twenty-six sail of the line manned and fit for the sea. Spain has seventeen sail in the same state, and more are fitting with such diligence, that they reckon to have thirty sail in each kingdom by April. This must have an immediate good effect in our favor, as it keeps the English fleet at bay, coops up their seamen, of whom they will scarce find sufficient to man their next set of transports, will probably keep Lord Howe's fleet more together, for fear of a visit, and leave us more sea room to prey upon their commerce, and a freer coast to bring in our prizes and supplies from abroad. The letter then mentions a circumstance [1] much to our advantage, but this is a secret. So strong is the inclination of the wealthy in France to assist us, that our Ambassadors have been offered a loan of two millions of livres, without interest, and to be repaid when the United States are settled in peace and prosperity. No conditions or securities are required. They have accepted this noble benefaction, and one half of it is paid into the hands of their Banker. On the strength of this supply, they are now in treaty for some strong ships.

Lee is in New York, confined, but otherwise treated well.

---

[1] The agreement made with the Farmers General to supply them with twenty thousand hogsheads of tobacco in America in payment for military stores.

LETTER CIV.[1]

Philadelphia, 3 April, 1777.

As you seem so inquisitive about politics, I will indulge you so far (indulge. I say. Observe that word,
indulge!—I suppose you will say, it ought to have
been, oblige,) as to send you a little more news from
abroad. As foreign affairs are now become more interesting to us than ever, I dare say, your political curiosity has extended itself, ere this, all over Europe.

The agent of the King of Prussia has often made
proposals of a commercial nature to our agents in
France, and expressed a desire that some American
would go to Berlin, at the instance of his sovereign,
who wishes to have a clear idea of the nature of our
commerce. You must know that this prince has been,
several years, dreaming of making his port of Emb-
den an Amsterdam. We cannot as yet depend, that
the Dutch merchants will venture to load directly to
America at their own risk. The States, however,
have declared, in answer to a fresh remonstrance of
General York, that their ports are open to all nations,
and that their trade, to and from their own colonies,
shall be unmolested, their subjects complying with the

---

[1] This letter is little more than an abstract of Mr. Silas
Deane's communications to the committee of secret correspondence, particularly that of the 1st of December, 1776. *Diplomatic Correspondence of the Revolution*, Vol. i. p. 77.

ordinances issued by their high mightinesses. Their prohibition of exporting warlike stores extends to all British subjects. Without a very material and apparent success of the British arms in America, a loan would be very slowly negotiated for England in Amsterdam. Nothing hinders them now from selling out of the English funds, but their not knowing what to do with the money. For that country may be called the treasury of Europe, and its stock of specie is more or less, according to the necessities of the different princes in Europe.

The credit of France has been very low of late. The mismanagement of the finances in the late King's reign, and the character of the late comptroller-general, M. de Clugny, had reduced it so low, that it was impossible to borrow anything considerable on perpetual funds. By life rents, something might be done. Perhaps a financier, in whose probity the world have a confidence, may restore their credit. The French stocks rose on the appointment of M. Taboureau. That it is possible for France to borrow, is certain, for at the time when M. Turgot was removed, he was negotiating a loan, and was likely to succeed, for sixty millions of guilders. The credit of Spain is extremely good. That kingdom may have what money it will, and on the best terms. The Emperor's credit is also good, not as Emperor, but from his hereditary dominions. Sweden and Denmark have good credit, the first the best. They have money at four per cent., and it is not long since the King of Sweden borrowed three millions of guilders at that interest, to pay off old debts at five per cent. His interest is paid punctually. Prussia has no credit, but his treasury is full by squeezing the last farthing from his people, and now and then he draws a little money from Holland, by reviving obsolete claims. The credit of the empress of Russia is very good, for she has punctually paid the interest of twelve millions of guilders, which she borrowed in her war with the Turk, and has lately paid off one million and a half of the principal. These are the strongest recommendations to a mercantile people. As to America, in the present state of affairs, it is not probable that a loan is practicable, but should it appear evident that we are likely to support our independency, or should either France or Spain acknowledge it, in either of these cases, we might have money, and when it shall be seen that we are punctual in our first payments of the interest, we shall have as much as we please.

LETTER CV.

Philadelphia, 6 April, 1777.

You have had many rumors propagated among you which I suppose you know not how to account for. One was, that Congress, the last summer, had tied the hands of General Washington, and would not let him fight, particularly on the White plains. This report was totally groundless. Another was, that at last, Congress untied the General, and then he instantly fought and conquered at Trenton. This also was without foundation, for as his hands were never tied, so they were not untied. Indeed, within a few days past, a question has been asked Congress, to the surprise, I believe, of every member there, whether the General was bound by the advice of a council of war? No member of Congress, that I know of, ever harbored or conceived such a thought. " Taking the advice of a council of war " are the words of the General's instructions, but this meant only, that councils of war should be called and their opinions and reasons demanded, but the General, like all other commanders of armies, was to pursue his own judgment after all.

Another report, which has been industriously circulated, is, that the General has been made by Congress, dictator. But this is as false as the other stories. Congress, it is true, upon removing to Baltimore, gave the General power to raise fifteen battalions, in addition to those which were ordered to be raised before, and to appoint the officers, and also, to raise three thousand horse, and to appoint their officers, and also, to take necessaries for his army, at an appraised value. But no more. Congress never thought of making him dictator, or of giving him a sovereignty. I wish I could find a correspondent, who was idle enough to attend to every report, and write it to me. Such false news, uncontradicted, does more or less harm. Such a collection of lies would be a curiosity for posterity.

The report you mention in your last, that the British administration had proposed to Congress a treaty and terms, is false, and without a color. On the contrary, it is now more than ever past a doubt, that their fixed determination is, conquest and unconditional subjugation. But there will be many words and blows too, before they will accomplish their wishes. Poor, abandoned, infatuated nation! Infatuation is one of the causes to which great historians ascribe many events, and if it ever produced any effect, it has produced this war against America.

Arnold, who carries this, was taken in his passage from Baltimore. He sailed with Harden for Boston. They took fifteen vessels while he was on board the man of war. Your flour was highly favored with good luck.

LETTER CVI.

[Philadelphia], 8 April, 1777.

YOURS of 26th March came by this day's post. I am happy to hear you have received so many letters from me. You need not fear writing in your cautious way, by the post, which is now well regulated. But if your letters should be intercepted, they would do no harm. The F.[1] turns out to be the man that I have

[1] Probably an allusion to the "Farmer," John Dickinson, who had been superseded in Congress on account of his oppo-

seen him to be these two years. He is in total neglect and disgrace here. I am sorry for it, because of
the forward part he took in the beginning of the controversy. But there is certainly such a thing as falling away in politics, if there is none in grace.

Lee fares as well as a man in close prison can fare,
I suppose, constantly guarded and watched. I fancy
Howe will engage that he shall be treated as a prisoner of war, and in that case we shall all be easy.
For my own part I don't think the cause depends
upon him. I am sorry to see such wild panegyrics
in your newspapers. I wish they would consider the
wars against idolatry.

11 April.

Congress is now full. Every one of the thirteen
States has a representation in it, which has not happened before a long time. Maryland has taken a
step which will soon complete their quota. They
have made it lawful for their officers to enlist servants
and apprentices.

The fine new frigate, called the *Delaware*, Captain
Alexander, has sailed down the river. I stood upon
the wharf to see the fine figure and show she made.
They are fitting away the *Washington*, Captain Reed,

sition to the Declaration of Independence. An extract from
a letter of his upon this subject will be found in " The Writings
of Washington," edited by Mr. Jared Sparks, Vol. iv. p. 291.
Note.

with all imaginable despatch. We have at last finished the system of officers for the Hospitals, which will be printed to-morrow. As soon as it is done, I will enclose it to you. A most ample, generous, liberal provision it is. The expense will be great, but humanity overcame avarice.

LETTER CVII.

[Philadelphia], Sunday, 13 April, 1777.

ENCLOSED with this, you have a correspondence[1] between the two Generals concerning the cartel for the exchange of prisoners. Washington is in the right, and has maintained his argument with a delicacy and dignity, which do him much honor. He has hinted at the flagitious conduct of the two Howes towards their prisoners in so plain and clear a manner that he cannot be misunderstood, but yet a decency and a delicacy are preserved, which is the more to be applauded, because the natural resentment of such atrocious cruelties renders it very difficult to avoid a more pointed language in describing them. They might, indeed, without much impropriety have been painted in crimson colors of a deeper die. If Mr. Howe's heart is not callous, what must be his feelings when

---

[1] This correspondence may be found in the fourth volume of the "Writings of Washington," edited by Mr. Sparks.

he recollects the starvings, the freezings, the pestilential diseases, with which he coolly and deliberately destroyed the lives of so many unhappy men! If his conscience is not seared, how will he bear its lashes when he remembers his breach of honor, his breach of faith, his offence against humanity and divinity, his neighbor, and his God (if he thinks there is any such Supreme Being,) in impairing health that he ought to have cherished, and in putting an end to lives that he ought to have preserved, and in choosing the most slow, lingering and torturing death that he could have devised. I charitably suppose, however, that he would have chosen the shortest course and would have put every man to the sword or bayonet, and thereby have put an end to their sufferings at once, if he could have done it without detection. But this would have been easily proved upon him, both by friends and enemies, whereas, by hunger, frost and disease he might commit the murders with equal certainty, and yet be able to deny that he had done it. He might lay it to hurry, to confusion, to the fault of commissaries and other officers; nay, might deny that they were starved, frozen, and infected. He was determined to put them out of the way and yet to deny it; to get rid of his enemies and yet save his reputation. But his reputation is ruined forever.

The two brothers will be ranked by posterity with Pizarro, with Borgia, with Alva, and with others in the annals of infamy, whose memories are entitled to the hisses and execrations of all virtuous men. These two unprincipled men are the more detestable, because

they were in the opposition at home, their connexions, friendships and interest lay with the opposition ;
to the opposition they owed their rise, promotion and
importance. Yet they have basely deserted their
friends and party, and have made themselves the servile tools of the worst of men in the worst of causes.
But what will not desperate circumstances tempt men
to do, who are without principle and who have a
strong, aspiring ambition, a towering pride and a tormenting avarice ? These two Howes were very poor,
and they have spent the little fortunes they had in
bribery at elections, and having obtained seats in Parliament, and having some reputation as brave men,
they had nothing to do but to carry their votes and
their valor to market, and, it is very true, they have
sold them at a high price.

Are titles of honor the reward of infamy ? Is gold
a compensation for vice ? Can the one or the other
give that pleasure to the heart, that comfort to the
mind, which it derives from doing good ? from a con-
sciousness of acting upon upright and generous principles, of promoting the cause of right, freedom and
the happiness of men ? Can wealth, or titles soften
the pains of the mind upon reflecting that a man has
done evil and endeavored to do evil to millions, that
he has destroyed free governments, and established ty-
rannies ? I would not be a Howe for all the empires
of the earth and all the riches and glories thereof.
Who would not rather be brave even though unfortunate in the cause of liberty ? who would not rather be
Sidney than Monk ?

However, if I am not deceived, misfortune as well as infamy awaits these men. They are doomed to defeat and destruction. It may take time to effect it, but it will certainly come. America is universally convinced of the necessity of meeting them in the field in firm battalion, and American fire is terrible.

LETTER CVIII.

[Philadelphia], 13 April, 1777.

I HAVE spent an hour this morning in the congregation of the dead. I took a walk into the Potter's field, a burying ground between the new stone prison and the hospital, and I never in my whole life was affected with so much melancholy. The graves of the soldiers, who have been buried in this ground from the hospital and bettering house during the course of the last summer, fall and winter, dead of the small pox and camp diseases, are enough to make the heart of stone to melt away. The sexton told me that upwards of two thousand soldiers had been buried there, and by the appearance of the graves and trenches, it is most probable to me, he speaks within bounds. To what causes this plague is to be attributed I don't know. It seems to me that the want of tents, clothes, soap, vegetables, vinegar, vaults, &c., cannot account for it all. Oat meal and peas are a great preservative of our enemies. Our frying pans and gridirons slay more than the sword. Discipline, discipline is the great thing wanted. There can be no order nor cleanliness in an army without discipline. We have at last determined on a plan for the sick, and have called into the service the best abilities in physic and chirurgery that the continent affords. I pray God it may have its desired effect, and that the lives and health of the soldiers may be saved by it. Disease has destroyed ten men for us, where the sword of the enemy has killed one.

Upon my return from my pensive, melancholy walk, I heard a piece of disagreeable news. That the ship *Morris*, Captain Anderson, from Nantes, with cannon, arms, gun-locks, powder, &c., was chased into Delaware Bay by two or three men of war ; that she defended herself manfully against their boats and barges, but finding no possibility of getting clear, she ran aground. The crew and two French gentlemen passengers got on shore, but the Captain, determined to disappoint his enemy in part, laid a train and blew up the ship, and lost his own life, unfortunately, in the explosion. I regret the loss of so brave a man much more than that of the ship and cargo. The people are fishing in order to save what they can, and I hope they will save the cannon. The French gentlemen, it is said, have brought despatches from France to the Congress. I hope this is true. If it is, I will let you know the substance of it, if I may be permitted to disclose it.

Philadelphia, 19 April, 1777.

WE have now an ample representation from New York.   It consists of six delegates, and they are to all appearance as high, as decisive, and as determined as any men ever were or can be.   There is a new hand, a Mr. Duer, who is a very fine fellow, a man of sense, spirit and activity, and is exceeded by no man in zeal.   Mr. Duane and Mr. Philip Livingston are apparently as determined as any men in Congress. You will see, by the enclosed newspapers, that Duane and Jay have arrived at the honor of being ranked with the two Adamses.   I hope they will be duly sensible of the illustrious distinction and be sure to behave in a manner becoming it.

This is the anniversary of the ever memorable 19th April, 1775.   Two complete years we have maintained open war with Great Britain and her allies, and after all our difficulties and misfortunes, are much abler to cope with them now than we were at the beginning.

[Philadelphia], 23 April, 1777.

My barber has just left the chamber. The¯following curious dialogue was the amusement during the gay moments of shaving.

" Well, Burne, what is the lie of the day ? " " Sir, Mr —— told me, that a privateer from Baltimore has taken two valuable prizes with sixteen guns each. I can scarcely believe it." " Have you heard of the success of the *Rattlesnake*, of Philadelphia, and the *Sturdy Beggar*, of Maryland, Mr. Burne ? These two privateers have taken eleven prizes, and sent them into the West India Islands ; nine transports and two guinea men." " Confound the ill luck, Sir ; I was going to sea myself on board the *Rattlesnake*, and my wife fell a yelping. These wives are queer things. I told her, I wondered she had no more ambition." " Now," says I, " when· you walk the streets and any body asks who that is ? The answer is " *Burne the barber's wife*." Should you not be better pleased to hear it said, " *That is Captain Burne's la-dy*," the captain of marines on board the Rattlesnake ? " " O," says she, " I would rather be called Burne the barber's wife, than Captain Burne's widow. I don 't desire to live better than you maintain me, my dear." So it is, Sir, by this sweet, honey language, I am choused out of my prizes, and must go on with my soap and razors and pincers and combs. I wish she had my ambition."

If this letter should be intercepted by the Tories, they will get a booty. Let them enjoy it. If some of their wives had been as tender and discreet as the barber's, their husbands' ambition would not have led them into so many salt ponds. What an *ignis fatuus* this ambition is? How few of either sex have arrived at Mrs. Burne's pitch of moderation, and are able to say, " I don't desire to live better, and had rather be the Barber's wife, than the Captain's widow "! Quite smart, I think, as well as philosophical.

LETTER CXI.

[Philadelphia], Saturday Evening, 26 April, 1777.

I HAVE been lately more remiss than usual in writing to you. There has been a great dearth of news. Nothing from England, nothing from France, Spain or any other part of Europe, nothing from the West Indies nothing from Howe and his banditti, nothing from General Washington. There are various conjectures that Lord Howe is dead, sick, or gone to England, as the proclamations run in the name of Will. Howe only, and nobody from New York can tell any thing of his lordship.

I am wearied out with expectations that the Massachusetts troops would have arrived, ere now, at Head
Quarters. Do our people intend to leave the continent in the lurch? Do they mean to submit? or
what fatality attends them? With the noblest prize
in view that ever mortals contended for, and with the
fairest prospect of obtaining it upon easy terms, the
people of the Massachusetts Bay are dead. Does our
state intend to send only half, or a third of their
quota? Do they wish to see another crippled, dis-
astrous and disgraceful campaign, for want of an
army? I am more sick and more ashamed of my
own countrymen, than ever I was before. The
spleen, the vapors, the dismals, the horrors seem to
have seized our whole state. More wrath than terror
has seized me. I am very mad. The gloomy
cowardice of the times is intolerable in New England.
Indeed I feel not a little out of humor from indis-
position of body. You know I cannot pass a spring,
or fall without an ill turn, and I have had one these
four or five weeks. A cold as usual. Warm weather
and a little exercise with a little medicine, I suppose,
will cure me, as usual. I am not confined, but mope
about and drudge, as usual, like a galley slave. I
am a fool, if ever there was one, to be such a slave.
I won't be much longer. I will be more free in
some world or other. Is it not intolerable, that the
opening spring, which I should enjoy with my wife
and children, upon my little farm, should pass away,
and laugh at me for laboring, day after day, and
month after month, in a conclave, where neither taste,

nor fancy, nor reason, nor passion, nor appetite can be gratified?

Posterity! you will never know how much it cost the present generation to preserve your freedom! I hope you will make a good use of it. If you do not, I shall repent in Heaven that I ever took half the pains to preserve it.

———

LETTER CXII.

[Philadelphia], 27 April, 1777.

YOUR favors of April 2d and 7th I have received. The enclosed Evening Post will give you some idea of the humanity of the present race of Britons. My barber, whom I quote as often as ever I did any authority, says, " he has read histories of cruelty and he has read romances of cruelty, but the cruelty of the British exceeds all that he ever read." For my own part I think we cannot dwell too much on this part of their character and conduct. It is full of important lessons. If the facts only were known, in the utmost simplicity of narration, they would strike every pious and humane bosom in Great Britain with horror. Every conscience in that country is not callous, nor every heart hardened. The plainest relation of facts would interest the sympathy and compassion of all Europe in our favor. And it would convince every

American, that a nation, so great a part of which is thus deeply depraved, can never be again trusted with power over us. I think that not only history should perform her office, but painting, sculpture, statuary and poetry ought to assist, in publishing to the world and perpetuating to posterity, the horrid deeds of our enemies. It will show the persecution we suffer in defence of our rights ; it will show the fortitude, patience, perseverance, and magnanimity of Americans, in as strong a light as the barbarity and impiety of Briton, in this persecuting war. Surely impiety consists in destroying with such hellish barbarity the rational works of the Deity, as much as in blaspheming and defying his majesty.

If there is a moral law, if there is a divine law, (and that there is, every intelligent creature is conscious,) to trample on these laws, to hold them in contempt and defiance is the highest exertion of wickedness and impiety that mortals can be guilty of. The author of human nature, who can give it its rights, will not see it ruined, and suffer its destroyers to escape with impunity. Divine vengeance will, sometime or other, overtake the Alberts, the Philips and Georges, the Alvas, the Grislers, and Howes, and vindicate the wrongs of oppressed human nature. I think that medals in gold, silver and copper ought to be struck in commemoration of the shocking cruelties, the brutal barbarities, and the diabolical impieties of this war ; and these should be contrasted with the kindness, tenderness, humanity and philanthropy which have marked the conduct of Americans towards their prisoners. It is remarkable that the officers and soldiers of our enemies are so totally depraved, so completely destitute of the sentiments of philanthropy in their own hearts, that they cannot believe that such delicate feelings can exist in any other, and therefore have constantly ascribed that milk and honey with which we have treated them, to fear, cowardice and conscious weakness. But in this they are mistaken, and will discover their mistake too late to answer any good purpose for them.

LETTER CXIII.

[Philadelphia], 23 April, 1777.

THERE is a clock calm at this time in the political and military hemispheres. The surface is smooth and the air serene. Not a breath nor a wave, no news nor noise.

Nothing would promote our cause more than Howe's march to this town. Nothing quickens and determines people so much as a little smart. The Germans, who are numerous and wealthy in this State, and who have very imperfect ideas of freedom, have a violent attachment to property. They are passionate and vindictive, in a degree that is scarcely credible to persons who are unacquainted with them, and the least injury to their property excites a resentment beyond description. A few houses and plantations plundered, (as many would be if Howe should come here,) would set them all on fire. Nothing would unite and determine Pennsylvania so effectually. The passions of men must coöperate with their reason in the prosecution of a war. The public may be clearly convinced, that a war is just, and yet, until their passions are excited, will carry it languidly on. The prejudices, the anger, the hatred of the English against the French contributes greatly to their valor and success. The British court and their officers have studied to excite the same passions in the breasts of their soldiers against the Americans, well knowing their powerful effects. We, on the contrary, have treated their characters with too much tenderness. The Howes, their officers, and soldiers too, ought to be held up to the contempt, derision, hatred and abhorrence of the populace in every State, and of the common soldiers in every army. It would give me no pain to see them burned or hanged in effigy, in every town and village.

LETTER CXIV.

[Philadelphia], 4 May, 1777.

ENCLOSED with this you will have an Evening Post containing some of the tender mercies of the barbarians to their prisoners. If there is a man, woman or child in America who can read these depositions without resentment and horror, that person has no soul, or a very wicked one. Their treatment of prisoners last year, added to an act of Parliament, which they have made, to enable them to send prisoners to England, to be there murdered with still more relentless cruelty in prisons, will bring our officers and soldiers to the universal resolution to *conquer or die*. This maxim " CONQUER OR DIE " never failed to raise a people who adopted it to the head of mankind. An express from Portsmouth, last night, brought us news of the arrival of arms and ordnance enough to enable us to take vengeance of these foes of human nature.

LETTER CXV.

[Philadelphia], 7 May, 1777.

WE have no news here, except what we get from your country. The privateers act with great spirit, and are blessed with remarkable success. Some merchant ships are arrived this week from Maryland. They were first chased by men of war in attempting to get into Chesapeake Bay. They ran from them and attempted Delaware Bay. There they were chased again, whereupon they again shifted their course for Chesapeake, and got in safe, in spite of all the men of war could do. Thus you see, we can and will have trade in spite of them, and this trade will probably increase fast. It requires time for the stream of commerce to alter its channel. Time is necessary for our merchants and foreign merchants to think, plan, and correspond with each other. Time, also, is necessary for our masters of vessels and mariners to become familiar with the coasts, forts and harbors of foreign countries, and a longer time still is needful for French, Spanish and Dutch masters and mariners to learn our coasts and harbors.

Yours ever, ever yours.

LETTER CXVI.

Philadelphia, 10 May, 1777.

THE day before yesterday, I took a walk with my friend Whipple to Mrs. Wells's, the sister of the famous Mrs. Wright,[1] to see her wax-work. She has two chambers filled with it. In one, the parable of the prodigal son is represented. The prodigal is

---

[1] Some account of Mrs. Wright, as a modeller in wax-work, may be found in Dunlap's " History of the rise and progress of the arts of design in the United States," Vol. i. p. 131. See also the " Letters of Mrs. Adams," Vol. II. p. 32.

prostrate on his knees before his father, whose joy and grief and compassion all appear in his eyes and face struggling with each other. A servant maid, at the father's command, is pulling down from a closet shelf the choicest robes to clothe the prodigal, who is all in rags. At an outward door in a corner of the room, stands the brother, chagrined at this festivity, a servant coaxing him to come in. A large number of guests are placed round the room. In another chamber are the figures of Chatham, Franklin, Sawbridge, Mrs. Macauley and several others. At a corner is a miser, sitting at his table weighing his gold, his bag upon one side of the table and a thief behind him endeavoring to pilfer the bag.

There is genius as well as taste and art discovered in this exhibition. But I must confess the whole scene was disagreeable to me. The imitation of life was too faint, and I seemed to be walking among a group of corpses, standing, sitting and walking, laughing, singing, crying and weeping. This art, I think, will make but little progress in the world.

Another historical piece, I forgot, which is Elisha restoring to life the Shunamite's son. The joy of the mother upon discovering the first symptoms of life in the child is pretty strongly expressed. Dr. Chevot's wax-work in which all the various parts of the human body are represented for the benefit of young students in anatomy, and of which I gave you a particular description a year or two ago, were much more pleasing to me. Wax is much fitter to represent dead bodies than living ones.

Upon a hint from one of our commissioners abroad, we are looking about for American curiosities to send across the Atlantic, as presents to the ladies. Mr. Rittenhouse's planetarium, Mr. Arnold's collection of varieties in the virtuoso way, which I once saw at Norwalk in Connecticut, Narraganset pacing mares, mooses, wood-ducks, flying squirrels, red-winged blackbirds, cranberries and rattlesnakes, have all been thought of. Is not this a pretty employment for great statesmen as we think ourselves to be? Frivolous as it seems, it may be of some consequence. Little attentions have great influence. I think, however, we ought to consult the ladies upon this point. Pray what is your opinion?

LETTER CXVII.

[Philadelphia], 15 May, 1777.

GENERAL WARREN writes me that my farm never looked better than when he last saw it, and that Mrs. —— was likely to outshine all the farmers. I wish I could see it. But I can make allowances. He knows the weakness of his friend's heart, and that nothing flatters it more than praises bestowed upon a certain lady. I am suffering every day for want of my farm to ramble in. I have been now for near ten weeks in a drooping, disagreeable way, constant y loaded with a cold. In the midst of infinite noise, hurry and bustle, I lead a lonely, melancholy life, mourning the loss of all the charms of life, which are my family, and all the amusements that I ever had in life, which is my farm. If the warm weather, which is now coming on, should not cure my cold, and make me better, I must come home. If it should, and I should get tolerably comfortable, I shall stay and reconcile myself to the misery I here suffer, as well as I can. I expect that I shall be chained to this oar until my constitution both of mind and body are totally destroyed and rendered wholly useless to myself and family for the remainder of my days.

However, now we have got over the dreary, dismal, torpid winter, when we had no army, not even three thousand men to protect us against all our enemies, foreign and domestic, and now we have got together a pretty respectable army, which renders us tolerably secure against both, I doubt not we shall be able to persuade some gentleman or other in the Massachusetts to vouchsafe to undertake the dangerous office of delegate to Congress. However, I will neither whine nor croak. The moment our affairs are in a prosperous way and a little more out of doubt, that moment I become a private gentleman, the respectful husband of the amiable Mrs. A., of B., and the affectionate father of her children, two characters which I have scarcely supported for these three years past, having done the duties of neither.

LETTER CXVIII.

Philadelphia, 17 May, 1777.

I NEVER fail to enclose to you the newspapers, which contain the most of the intelligence that comes to my knowledge. I am obliged to slacken my attention to business a little, and ride and walk for the sake of my health, which is but infirm. O! that I could wander upon Penn's hill and in the meadows and mountains in its neighborhood, free from care! But this is a felicity too great for me.

Mr. Gorham and Mr. Russel are here with a petition from Charlestown. It grieves me that they are to return without success. I feel, most exquisitely, for the unhappy people of that town. Their agents have done every thing in their power or in the power of men to do, and the Massachusetts delegates have seconded their efforts to the utmost of their power, but all in vain. The distress of the States, arising from the quantity of money abroad, and the monstrous demands that would be made from Virginia, New Jersey, New York and elsewhere, if a precedent should be once set, has determined the Congress, almost with tears in their eyes, to withstand this application at present. Every man expressed the utmost tenderness and humanity upon the occasion: but at the same time, every man, except the Massachusetts delegates, expressed his full conviction of the ill policy of granting any thing at present.

LETTER CXIX.

[Philadelphia], 22 May, 4 o'clock in the morning.

AFTER a series of the severest and harshest weather
that ever I felt in this climate, we are at last blessed
with a bright sun and a soft air. The weather here
has been like our old easterly winds to me and south-
erly winds to you. The charms of the morning at
this hour are irresistible. The streaks of glory dawn-
ing in the east; the freshness and purity in the air,
the bright blue of the sky, the sweet warblings of a
great variety of birds intermingling with the martial
clarions of a hundred cocks now within my hearing,
all conspire to cheer the spirits.

This kind of puerile description is a very pretty employment for an old fellow whose brow is furrowed
with the cares of politics and war. I shall be on
horseback in a few minutes and then I shall enjoy the
morning in more perfection. I spent last evening at
the war office with General Arnold. He has been
basely slandered and libelled. The regulars say,
" he fought like Julius Cæsar."[1] I am wearied to

[1] At Danbury. The Congress had a short time before promoted several officers over his head. He was now made a Major General, and a horse, properly caparisoned, was presented
to him for his bravery, by a formal vote. See *Journals for* 20th
May, 1777. Also " *The Writings of Washington*," Vol. iv. pp.
377, 408.

death with the wrangles between military officers, high and low. They quarrel like cats and dogs. They worry one another like mastiffs, scrambling for rank and pay, like apes for nuts. I believe there is no one principle which predominates in human nature so much, in every stage of life, from the cradle to the grave, in males and females, old and young, black and white, rich and poor, high and low, as this passion for superiority. Every human being compares itself in its imagination with every other round about it, and will find some superiority over every other, real or imaginary, or it will die of grief and vexation. I have seen it among boys and girls at school, among lads at college, among practitioners at the bar, among the clergy in their associations, among clubs of friends, among the people in town meetings, among the members of a House of Representatives, among the grave councillors, on the more solemn bench of Justice, and in that awfully august body, the Congress, and on many of its committees, and among ladies every where; but I never saw it operate with such keenness, ferocity and fury, as among military officers. They will go terrible lengths in their emulation, their envy and revenge, in consequence of it.

So much for philosophy. I hope my five or six babes are all well. My duty to my mother and your father, and love to sisters and brothers, aunts and uncles. Pray how does your asparagus perform? &c. I would give three guineas for a barrel of your cider. Not one drop is to be had here for gold, and wine is not to be had under six or eight dollars a gallon, and that

very bad. I would give a guinea for a barrel of
your beer. The small beer here is wretchedly bad.
In short, I can get nothing that I can drink, and I believe I shall be sick from this cause alone. Rum at
forty shillings a gallon, and bad water will never do,
in this hot climate, in summer, when acid liquors are
necessary against putrefaction.

LETTER CXX.

[Philadelphia], 25 May, 1777.

At half past four this morning I mounted my horse
and took a ride in a road that was new to me. I
went to Kensington and then to " Point-no-point" by
land, the place where I went once before with a large
company in the row galleys by water. That frolic
was almost two years ago. I gave you a relation of
it in the time, I suppose. The road to Point-no-point
lies along the river Delaware, in fair sight of it and
its opposite shore. For near four miles the road is
as strait as the streets of Philadelphia. On each side,
are beautiful rows of trees, buttonwoods, oaks, wal-
nuts, cherries and willows, especially down towards
the banks of the river. The meadows, pastures and
grass plats are as green as leeks. There are many
fruit trees and fine orchards set with the nicest

regularity. But the fields of grain, the rye and wheat exceed all description. These fields are all sown in ridges and the furrow between each couple of ridges is as plainly to be seen as if a swath had been mown along. Yet it is no wider than a ploughshare and it is as strait as an arrow. It looks as if the sower had gone along the furrow with his spectacles to pick up every grain that should accidentally fall into it. The corn is just coming out of the ground. The furrows struck out for the hills to be planted in, are each way as straight, as mathematical right lines; and the squares between every four hills as exact as they could be done by plumb and line, or scale and compass.

I am ashamed of our farmers. They are a lazy, ignorant set; in husbandry, I mean ; for they know infinitely more of every thing else than these. But after all, the native face of our country, diversified as it is with hill and dale, sea and land, is to me more agreeable than this enchanting artificial scene.

27 May.

The post brought me yours of May 6th and 9th. You express apprehensions that we may be driven from this city. We have no such apprehensions here. Howe is unable to do any thing but by stealth. Washington is strong enough to keep Howe where he is.

How could it happen that you should have £5 counterfeit New Hampshire money ? Can 't you recollect who you had it of? Let me entreat you not to take a shilling of any but continental money or Massachusetts, and be very careful of that. There is a counterfeit continental bill abroad sent out of New York, but it will deceive none but fools, for it is copper plate, easily detected, miserably done.

———

LETTER CXXI.

[Philadelphia], Monday 2 June, 1777.

ARTILLERY Election! I wish I was at it or near it. Yours of the 18th reached me this morning. The cause that letters are so long in travelling is, that there is but one post in a week, who goes from hence to Peekskill, although there are two that go from thence to Boston. Riding every day has made me better than I was, although I am not yet quite well. I am determined to continue this practice, which is very necessary for me.

I rejoice to find that the town have had the wisdom to send but one Representative. The House last year was too numerous and unwieldy. The expense was too great. I suppose you will have a constitution formed this year. Who will be the Moses, the Lycurgus, the Solon? or have you a score or two of such? Whoever they may be, and whatever form may be adopted, I am persuaded there is among the mass of our people a fund of wisdom, integrity and humanity, which will preserve their happiness in a tolerable measure.

If the enemy comes to Boston again, fly with your little ones, all of them to Philadelphia. But they will scarcely get to Boston this campaign. I admire your sentiments concerning revenge. Revenge in ancient days, (you will see it through the whole Roman History) was esteemed a generous and an heroic passion. Nothing was too good for a friend, or too bad for an enemy. Hatred and malice without limits against an enemy were indulged, were justified, and no cruelty was thought unwarrantable. Our Saviour taught the immorality of revenge, and the moral duty of forgiving injuries, and even the duty of loving enemies. Nothing can shew the amiable, the moral, the divine excellency of these Christian doctrines in a stronger point of light than the characters and conduct of Marius and Sylla, Cæsar, Pompey, Antony and Augustus, among innumerable others. Retaliation we must practise in some instances, in order to make our barbarous foes respect, in some degree, the rights of humanity. But this will never be done without the most palpable necessity. The apprehension of retaliation alone will restrain them from cruelties which would disgrace savages. To omit it then would be cruelty to ourselves, our officers and men.

We are amused here with reports of troops removing from Rhode Island, New York, Staten Island, &c; waggons, boats, bridges, &c., prepared; two old Indiamen cut down into floating batteries, mounting

thirty-two guns, sent round into Delaware river, &c.,
&c; but I heed it no more than the whistling of the
zephyrs.   In short, I had rather they should come to
Philadelphia than not.   It would purify this city of
its dross.   Either the furnace of affliction would refine it of its impurities, or it would be purged yet so
as by fire.   This town has been a dead weight upon
us.   It would be a dead weight upon the enemy.
The mules here would plague them more than all
their money.

LETTER CXXII.

Philadelphia, 4 June, 1777.

I wish I could know whether your season is cold or
warm, wet or dry, fruitful or barren; whether you
had late frosts, whether those frosts have hurt the
fruit, the flax, the corn or vines, &c.   We have a fine
season here and a bright prospect of abundance.

You will see, by the enclosed papers in a letter
from my friend Parsons, a very handsome narration of
one of the prettiest exploits of this war, a fine retaliation of the Danbury mischief.   Meigs, who was before esteemed a good officer, has acquired, by this expedition, a splendid reputation.   You will see, by the
same papers, too, that the writers here in opposition to
the constitution of Pennsylvania are making factious

use of my name and lucubrations; much against my will, I assure you, for although I am no admirer of the form of this government, yet I think it is agreeable to the body of the people, and if they please themselves, they will please me.   And I would not choose to be impressed into the service of one party or the other, and I am determined I will not enlist.   Besides, it is not very genteel in these writers to put my name to a letter[1] from which I cautiously withheld it myself.   However, let them take their own way, I shall not trouble myself about it.

I am growing better by exercise and air.

———

LETTER CXXIII.

Philadelphia, 8 July, 1777.

YOURS of 23d June I have received.   I believe there is no danger of an invasion your way, but the designs of the enemy are uncertain, and their motions a little mysterious.   Before this letter is sealed, which will not be till Sunday next, I hope I shall be able to inform you better.

---

[1] "Thoughts on Government."   As this letter to Mr. Wythe has been frequently alluded to, and is not without interest as a memorial of the first steps taken towards framing the State Governments, it has been placed in the Appendix to the present volume,   B.

I rejoice at your fine season and at my brother Cranch's attention to husbandry. I am very glad he bought the farm and that he likes it so well. I pant for domestic life and rural felicity like his. I am better than I have been. But I dread the heats which are coming on. This day completes six months since I left you. I am wasted and exhausted in mind and body, with incessant applications to business, but if I can possibly endure it, will hold out the year. It is nonsense to dance backwards and forwards. After this year, I shall take my leave.

Our affairs are in a fine prosperous train, and if they continue so, I can leave this station with honor. Next month completes three years that I have been devoted to the service of liberty. A slavery it has been to me, whatever the world may think of it. To a man whose attachments to his family are as strong as mine, absence alone from such a wife and such children would be a great sacrifice. But in addition to this separation what have I not done? What have I not suffered? What have I not hazarded? These are questions that I may ask you, but I will ask such questions of none else. Let the cymbals of popularity tinkle still. Let the butterflies of fame glitter with their wings. I shall envy neither their music nor their colors. The loss of property affects me little. All other hard things I despise, but the loss of your company and that of my dear babes for so long a time, I consider as a loss of so much solid happiness. The tender social feelings of my heart which have distressed me beyond all utterance in my most busy active scenes as well as in the numerous hours of melancholy solitude, are known only to God and my own soul.

How often have I seen my dearest friend, a widow, and her charming prattlers, orphans exposed to all the insolence of unfeeling, impious tyrants! Yet I can appeal to my final Judge, the horrid vision has never for one moment shaken the resolution of my heart.

LETTER CXXIV.

Philadelphia, 11 July, 1777.

THIS letter will go by the hand of the Honorable Joseph Hewes, Esquire, one of the delegates in Congress from North Carolina from the month of September 1774, until 1777. I had the honor to serve with him upon the naval committee who laid the first foundations, the corner stone of an American navy, by fitting to sea the Alfred, Columbus, Cabot, Andrew Doria, Providence, and several others. An honor that I make it a rule to boast of upon all occasions and I hope my posterity will have reason to boast. Hewes has a sharp eye and keen penetrating sense, but, what is of much more value, is a man of honor and integrity. If he should call upon you, and you should be about, I hope you will treat him with all the complaisance that is due to his character. I almost envy him his journey, although he travels for his health, which at present is infirm.

I am, yours, yours, yours,

JOHN ADAMS.

MY DEAREST FRIEND,

We have had no news from camp for three or four days. Mr. Howe, by the last advices, was manœuvring his fleet and army in such a manner as give us expectations of an expedition, somewhere ; but whether to Rhode Island, Halifax, up the North River, or the Delaware, is left to conjecture. I am much in doubt whether he knows his own intentions. A faculty of penetrating into the designs of an enemy is said to be the first quality of a general, but it is impossible to discover the designs of an enemy who has no design at all. An intention that has no existence, a plan that is not laid, cannot be divined. Be his intentions what they may, you have nothing to fear from him. He has not force to penetrate the country any where.

LETTER CXXV.

Philadelphia, 13 July, 1777.

MY DEAREST FRIEND,

WE have a confused account from the northward of something unlucky at Ticonderoga, but cannot certainly tell what it is. I am much afraid we shall lose that post, as we did forts Washington and Lee ; and indeed, I believe we shall, if the enemy surround it. But it will prove no benefit to him. I begin to wish there was not a fort upon the continent. Discipline and disposition are our resources. It is our policy to draw the enemy into the country, where we can avail ourselves of hills, woods, rivers, defiles, &c., until our soldiers are more inured to war. Howe and Burgoyne will not be able to meet this year, and if they were met, it would only be better for us, for we should draw all our forces to a point too. If they were met, they could not cut off the communication between the northern and southern States. But if the communication was cut off for a time, it would be no misfortune, for New England would defend itself, and the southern States would defend themselves.

Colonel Miles is come out of New York on his parole. His account is, as I am informed, that Mr. Howe's projects are all deranged. His army has gone round the circle, and is now encamped in the very spot where he was a year ago. The spirits of the Tories are sunk to a great degree, and those of the army too. The Tories have been elated with prospects of coming to this city and triumphing, but are miserably disappointed. The Hessians are disgusted, and their general de Heister gone home in a miff.

LETTER CXXVI.

[Philadelphia], 11 August, 1777.

YOUR kind favor of July 30th and 31st,[1] was handed
me just now from the post office. I have regularly
received a letter from you, every week excepting one,
for a long time past, and as regularly send a line to
you enclosing papers. My letters are scarcely worth
sending. Indeed I don't choose to indulge much
speculation, lest a letter should miscarry, and free
sentiments upon public affairs intercepted from me
might do much hurt.

Where the scourge of God and the plague of mankind is gone, no one can guess. An express from
Sinnepuxent, a place between the Capes of Delaware
and the Capes of Chesapeake, informs, that a fleet of
one hundred sail was seen off that place last Thursday. But whether this is fishermen's news, like that
from Cape Ann, I know not. The time spends, and
the campaign wears away, and Howe makes no great
figure yet. How many men and horses will he crip-
ple by this strange coasting voyage of five weeks?

We have given New England men what they will
think a complete triumph in the removal of Generals
from the northward and sending Gates there. I hope
every part of New England will now exert itself to

[1] Letters of Mrs. Adams, Vol. I. p. 110.

its utmost efforts. Never was a more glorious opportunity than Burgoyne has given us of destroying him by marching down so far towards Albany. Let New England turn out and cut off his retreat. Pray, continue to write me every week. You have made me merry with the female frolic with the miser. But I hope the females will leave off their attachment to coffee. I assure you the best families in this place have left off, in a great measure, the use of West India goods. We must bring ourselves to live upon the produce of our own country. What would I give for some of your cider? Milk has become the breakfast of many of the wealthiest and genteelest families here.

Fenno put me into a kind of frenzy to go home, by the description he gave me, last night, of the fertility of the season, the plenty of fish, &c., &c., &c., in Boston and about it. I am condemned to this place, a miserable exile from every thing that is agreeable to me. God will my banishment shall not last long.

LETTER CXXVII.

Philadelphia, 11 August, 1777.

MY DEAREST FRIEND,

I THINK I have sometimes observed to you in conversation, that upon examining the biography of illustrious men, you will generally find some female about

them, in the relation of mother, or wife, or sister, to
whose instigation a great part of their merit is to be
ascribed.   You will find a curious example of this in
the case of Aspasia, the wife of Pericles.   She was a
woman of the greatest beauty and the first genius.
She taught him, it is said, his refined maxims of policy, his lofty imperial eloquence, nay, even composed
the speeches on which so great a share of his reputation was founded.   The best men in Athens frequent-
ed her house and brought their wives to receive lessons from her of economy and right deportment.
Socrates himself was her pupil in eloquence, and gives
her the honor of that funeral oration, which he deliv-
ers in the Menexenus of Plato.   Aristophanes, indeed, abuses this famous lady, but Socrates does her
honor.

I wish some of our great men had such wives.   By
the account in your last letter, it seems the women in
Boston begin to think themselves able to serve their
country.   What a pity it is, that our generals in the
northern districts had not Aspasias to their wives !

I believe the two Howes have not very great women for wives.   If they had, we should suffer more
from their exertions than we do.   This is our good
fortune.   A woman of good sense would not let her
husband spend five weeks at sea in such a season of
the year.   A smart wife would have put Howe in possession of Philadelphia, a long time ago.

Philadelphia, Tuesday, 19 August, 1777.

MY BEST FRIEND,

YOUR obliging favor of the 5th[1] came by yesterday's post, and I intended to have answered it by this morning's post, but was delayed by many matters, until he gave me the slip.

I am sorry that you and the people of Boston were put to so much trouble, but glad to hear that such numbers determined to fly. The prices for carting which were demanded were detestable. I wish your fatigue and anxiety may not have injured your health. Don't be anxious for my safety. If Howe comes here, I shall run away, I suppose, with the rest. We are too brittle ware, you know, to stand the dashing of balls and bombs. I wonder upon what principle the Roman senators refused to fly from the Gauls, and determined to sit with their ivory staves and hoary beards, in the porticoes of their houses, until the enemy entered the city and, although they confessed they resembled the gods, put them to the sword. I should not choose to indulge this sort of dignity; but I confess I feel myself so much injured by these barbarian Britons, that I have a strong inclination to meet them in the field. This is not revenge, I believe, but there is something sweet and delicious in the contemplation

---

[1] Letters of Mrs. Adams, Vol. I. p. 113.

of it. There is in our hearts an indignation against wrong that is righteous and benevolent ; and he who is destitute of it, is defective in the balance of his affections and in his moral character.

As long as there is conscience in our breasts, a moral sense which distinguishes between right and wrong, approving, esteeming, loving the former, and undermining and detesting the other, we must feel a pleasure in the punishment of so eminent a contemner of all that is right, and good, and just, as Howe is. They are virtuous and pious passions that prompt us to desire his destruction, and to lament and deplore his success and prosperity. The desire of assisting towards his disgrace is an honest wish.

It is too late in life, my constitution is too much debilitated by speculation, and indeed, it is too late a period in the war, for me to think of girding on a sword. But if I had the last four years to run over again, I certainly would.

LETTER CXXIX.

Philadelphia, Tuesday, 19 August, 1777.

MY BEST FRIEND,

THE weather still continues cloudy and cool, and the wind easterly. Howe's fleet and army is still incognito. The gentlemen from South Carolina begin to tremble for Charleston. If Howe is under a judicial blindness, he may be gone there. But what will be the fate of a scorbutic army, cooped up in a fleet for six, seven, or eight weeks, in such intemperate weather as we have had ? What will be their condition, landing on a burning shore abounding with agues and musquetoes, in the most unwholesome season of the whole year ? If he should get Charleston, or indeed the whole State, what progress will this make towards the conquest of America ? He will stop the trade of rice and indigo, but what then ? Besides, he will get some ugly knocks. They are honest, sincere, and brave, and will make his life uncomfortable.

I feel a strong affection for South Carolina for several reasons. 1. I think them as stanch patriots as any in America. 2. I think them as brave. 3. They are the only people in America, who have maintained a post and defended a fort. 4. They have sent us a new delegate whom I greatly admire, Mr. Laurens, their Lieutenant Governor, a gentleman of great fortune, great abilities, modesty and integrity, and great experience too. If all the States would send us such men, it would be a pleasure to be here.

In the northern department they begin to fight. The family of Johnson, the black part of it as well as the white are pretty well thinned. Rascals ! They deserve extermination. I presume Gates will be so supported that Burgoyne will be obliged to retreat. He will stop at Ticonderoga, I suppose, for they can maintain posts although we cannot. I think we shall never defend a post until we shoot a general. After that we shall defend posts, and this event in my opin-

ion is not far off. No other fort will ever be evacua-
ted without an inquiry, nor any officer come off without a court martial. We must trifle no more. We
have suffered too many disgraces to pass unexpiated.
Every disgrace must be wiped off.

We have been several days hammering upon money. We are contriving every way we can to redress the evils we feel and fear from too great a quantity of paper. Taxation as deep as possible is the
only radical cure. I hope you will pay every tax that
is brought you, if you sell my books, or clothes, or
oxen, or your cows to pay it.

LETTER CXXX.

Philadelphia, Wednesday, 20 August, 1777.

MY BEST FRIEND,

THIS day completes three years since I stepped into
the coach at Mr. Cushing's door, in Boston, to go to
Philadelphia in quest of adventures. And adventures
I have found. I feel an inclination sometimes to write
the history of the last three years, in imitation of
Thucydides. There is a striking resemblance in several particulars between the Peloponnesian and the
American war. The real motive to the former was a
jealousy of the growing power of Athens by sea and
land. The genuine motive to the latter was a similar

jealousy of the growing power of America. The true causes which incite to war are seldom professed or acknowledged.

We are now upon a full sea: when we shall arrive at a safe harbor, no mariner has skill and experience enough to foretell. But by the favor of Heaven, we shall make a prosperous voyage, after all the storms and shoals are passed.

5 o'clock. Afternoon.

It is now fair sunshine again and very warm. Not a word yet from Howe's fleet. The most general suspicion now is, that it is gone to Charleston, South Carolina. But it is a wild supposition. It may be right however, for he is a wild General.

We have been hammering to-day upon a mode of trial for the general officers at Ti. Whether an inquiry will precede the court martial, and whether the inquiry shall be made by a committee of Congress, or by a council of general officers, is not determined, but inquiry and trial both, I conjecture there will be.

If Howe is gone to Charleston, you will have a little quiet, and enjoy your corn, and rye, and flax, and hay, and other good things, until another summer. But what shall we do for sugar and wine and rum? Why truly, I believe we must leave them off. Loaf sugar is only four dollars a pound here, and brown only a dollar for the meanest sort, and ten shillings for that a little better. Every body here is leaving off loaf sugar, and most are laying aside brown. As to rum and wine, give me cider and I would compound. New England rum is but forty shillings a gallon. But if wine was ten dollars a bottle I would have one glass a day in water while the hot weather continues, unless I could get cider.

LETTER CXXXI.

Philadelphia, Thursday, 21 August, 1777.

MY BEST FRIEND,

THIS morning we have heard again from the fleet. At nine o'clock at night on the fourteenth instant, upwards of a hundred sail were seen standing in between the capes of Chesapeake bay. They had been seen from the eastern shore of Virginia, standing off and on, for two days before. This method of coasting along the shore, and standing off and on, is very curious. First, seen off Egg harbor, then several times, off the capes of Delaware, standing in and out, then off Sinnepuxent, then off the eastern shore of Virginia, then standing in to Chesapeake bay. How many men and horses will he lose in this sea ramble, in the heat of dog days? Whether he is going to Virginia to steal tobacco, to North Carolina to pilfer pitch and tar, or to South Carolina to plunder rice and indigo, who can tell? He will seduce a few negroes from their masters, let him go to which he will. But is this conquering America?

From the northward we learn that Arnold has marched with about two thousand men to the relief of fort Schuyler. Our people have given Sir John Johnson and his regulars, Tories and Indians, a very fine drubbing. The Indians scarcely ever had such a mauling. The devils are so frightened that they are all run away to howl and mourn. The papers enclosed with this will give you more particular information. Can nothing be done at Rhode Island at this critical time? Opprobrium Novangliæ! What is become of all the Massachusetts continental troops? Every regiment and every man of them is at the northward under Gates, and yet we are told they have not four thousand men fit for duty, officers included. And there are three regiments there from New Hampshire too.

10 o'clock at night.

Just come in from Congress. We have within this hour received letters of General Schuyler and Lincoln, giving an account of the battle of Bennington, wherein General Stark has acquired great glory, and so have his militia. The particulars are to be out in a handbill to-morrow morning. I will enclose you one.

LETTER CXXXII.

Philadelphia, 23 August, 1777.

MY BEST FRIEND,

IT is now no longer a secret where Mr. Howe's fleet is. We have authentic intelligence that it is arrived at the head of Chesapeake bay, above the river Patapsco, upon which the town of Baltimore stands. I wish I could describe to you the geography of this country, so as to give you an adequate idea of the situation of the two great bays of Chesapeake and Delaware, because it would enable you to form a conjecture concerning the object he aims at. The distance across land from the heads of these bays is but small, and forms an isthmus, below which is a large peninsula, comprehending the counties of Accomac and Northampton in Virginia, the counties of Somerset and Worcester in Maryland, and the counties of Kent and Sussex in Delaware. His march by land to Philadelphia may be about sixty or seventy miles. I think there can be no doubt that he aims at this place, and he has taken this voyage of six weeks, long enough to have gone to London, merely to avoid an army in his rear. He found he could not march this way from Somerset court house without leaving General Washington in his rear. We have called out the militia of Virginia, Maryland, Delaware and Pennsylvania, to oppose him, and General Washington is handy enough to meet him ; and as General Washington saved Philadelphia last winter by crossing the Delaware and marching to Morristown, and so getting in the rear of Howe, so, I conjecture, he will still find means to get in his rear between him and Chesapeake bay. You may now sit under your own vine and have none to make you afraid. I sent off my man and horse at an unlucky time, but if we should be obliged to remove from hence, we shall not go far.

If Congress had deliberated and debated a month, they could not have concerted a plan for Mr. Howe more to our advantage, than that which he has adopted. He gives us an opportunity of exerting the strength of all the middle States against him, while New York and New England are destroying Burgoyne. Now is the time ! never was so good an opportunity for my countrymen to turn out and crush that vaporing, blustering bully to atoms.

LETTER CXXXIII.

Philadelphia, Saturday, 23 August, 1777, 4 o'clock.

MY BEST FRIEND,

WE have an express to-day from Governor Johnson, Captain Nicholson and several other gentlemen, with an account that the fleet, to the number of two hundred and sixty-three sail, have gone up towards the

head of Chesapeake bay. They lie over against the
shore between the river Sassafras and the river Elk.
We have also a letter from General Washington acquainting us, that to-morrow morning at seven o'clock,
he shall march his army through the city of Philadelphia, along Front street, and then turn up Chestnut
street in his way to cross over the bridge at Schuylkill
river; so that General Howe will have a grand continental army to oppose him, in very good season,
aided by a formidable collection of militia. I like
this movement of the General through the city. Such
a show of artillery, waggons, light horse and infantry,
which takes up a line of nine or ten miles upon their
march, and will not be less than five or six hours passing through the town, will make a good impression
upon the minds of the timorous whigs for their con-
firmation; upon the cunning Quakers for their restraint; and upon the rascally Tories for their confusion.

I think there is a reasonable ground for confidence,
with the favor of Heaven, that Howe will not be able to
reach this city. Yet I really doubt whether it would
not be more for our interest that he should come here,
and get possession of the town.

1. Because there are impurities here which will
never be so soon or so fully purged away, as by that
fire of affliction which Howe enkindles wherever he
goes.

2. Because it would employ nearly the whole of
his force to keep possession of this town, and the rest
of the continent would be more at liberty.

3. We could counteract him here, better than in many other places.

4. He would leave New England and New York at leisure to kill or catch Burgoyne.

In all events you may rejoice and sing, for the season is so far gone that he cannot remove to you.

———

LETTER CXXXIV.

Philadelphia, 24 August, 1777.

MY DEAREST FRIEND,

WE had, last evening, a thunder gust very sharp and violent, attended with a plentiful rain. The lightning struck in several places. It struck the Quaker almshouse in Walnut street, between Third and Fourth streets, not far from Captain Duncan's, where I lodge. They had been wise enough to place an iron rod upon the top of the steeple, for a vane to turn on, and had provided no conductor to the ground. It also struck in Fourth street, near Mrs. Cheesman's. No person was hurt.

This morning was fair, but now it is overcast and rains very hard, which will spoil our show, and wet the army.

12 o'clock.

The rain ceased, and the army marched through the town between seven and ten o'clock. The wag-

gons went another road. Four regiments of light
horse, Bland's, Baylor's, Sheldon's and Moylan's.
Four grand divisions of the army, and the artillery
with the matrosses. They marched twelve deep, and
yet took up above two hours in passing by. General
Washington and the other general officers with their
aids on horseback. The Colonels and other field officers on horseback. We have now an army well
appointed between us and Mr. Howe, and this army
will be immediately joined by ten thousand militia, so
that I feel as secure here as if I was at Braintree, but
not so happy. My happiness is nowhere to be found
but there.

After viewing this fine spectacle and firm defence,
I went to Mr. Duffield's meeting to hear him pray, as
he did most fervently, and I believe he was most sincerely joined by all present, for its success.

The army, upon an accurate inspection of it, I find
to be extremely well armed, pretty well clothed and
tolerably disciplined. Gill and Town, by the motto
to their newspapers, will bring discipline into vogue in
time. There is such a mixture of the sublime and
the beautiful together with the useful in military discipline, that I wonder every officer we have is not
charmed with it. Much remains yet to be done. Our
soldiers have not yet quite the air of soldiers. They
don't step exactly in time. They don't hold up their
heads quite erect, nor turn out their toes so exactly
as they ought. They don't all of them cock their
hats, and such as do, don't all wear them the same
way.

A disciplinarian has affixed to him commonly the ideas of cruelty, severity, tyranny, &c. But if I were an officer, I am convinced I should be the most decisive disciplinarian in the army. I am convinced there is no other effective way of indulging benevolence, humanity, and the tender social passions in an army. There is no other way of preserving the health and spirits of the men. There is no other way of making them active and skilful in war; no other way of guarding an army against destruction by surprises, and no other method of giving them confidence in one another, or making them stand by one another in the hour of battle. Discipline in an army is like the laws in civil society. There can be no liberty in a commonwealth where the laws are not revered, and most sacredly observed, nor can there be happiness or safety in an army for a single hour where the discipline is not observed.

Obedience is the only thing wanting now for our salvation. Obedience to the laws in the States, and obedience to officers in the army.

12 o'clock.

No express nor accidental news from Maryland to-day, as yet.

Philadelphia, 25 August, 1775.

Yours of August 12th and 13th came by this morning's post. A letter from Chesapeake bay, dated yesterday morning, informs that the enemy had not then landed. This morning, General Nash, with his brigade of North Carolina forces, marched through the town with their band of music, their train of artillery and their baggage waggons, their bread waggons, travelling forges, &c. General Washington's army encamped last night at Derby. Sullivan's division is expected along in two days. Our intelligence of the fleet has been as good as could be expected. They have been six weeks at sea.

If our people do not now turn out and destroy Burgoyne's gang, root and branch, they may justly be reproached as lost to honor and to virtue. He is completely in our power. Gates writes to Congress that Burgoyne is lessened twelve hundred men by the Bennington action.

LETTER CXXXVI.

Philadelphia, Tuesday, 26 August, 1777.

MY BEST FRIEND,

Howe's army, at least about five thousand of them, besides his light horse, are landed upon the banks of the Elk river, and the disposition he has made of his forces indicates a design to rest and refresh both men and horses. General Washington was at Wilmington last night, and his army is there to-day. The militia are turning out with great alacrity both in Maryland and Pennsylvania. They are distressed for want of arms. Many have none, others have only little fowling pieces. However, we shall rake and scrape enough to do Howe's business, by the favor of Heaven.

Howe must have intended that Washington should have sent his army up to fight Burgoyne. But he is disappointed. The kindness of Heaven towards us has in nothing appeared more conspicuous, than in this motion of Howe. If the infatuation is not so universal as to seize Americans as well as him, it will prove the certain destruction of Burgoyne's army. The New England troops and New York troops are every man of them at Peekskill and with Gates. The Massachusetts men are all with Gates. General Washington has none but southern troops with him, and he has much the largest army to encounter.

If my countrymen do not now turn out and do

something, I shall be disappointed indeed.   One fifth
part of Burgoyne's army has been totally destroyed
by Stark and Herkimer.   The remainder must be
shocked and terrified at the stroke.   Now is the time
to strike.   New England men! strike home.

LETTER CXXXVII.

Philadelphia, Friday, 29 August, 1777.

MY DEAREST FRIEND,

THE newspapers enclosed will give you all the intelligence of any consequence.   General Washington, with
a very numerous army, is between Wilmington and
the Head of Elk.   Howe will make but a pitiful figure.
The militia of four States are turning out with much
alacrity and cheerful spirits.   The continental army
under Washington, Sullivan and Nash, besides, is in
my opinion more numerous by several thousands than
Howe's whole force.   I am afraid that he will be
frightened, and run on board his ships, and go away
plundering to some other place.   I almost wish he had
Philadelphia, for then he could not get away.   I really
think it would be the best policy to retreat before
him, and let him into this snare, where his army must
be ruined.   However, this policy will not be adopted.

In a letter from good authority, Mr. Paca, we are
informed that many dead horses have been driven on

the eastern shore of Maryland. Horses thrown over-
board from the fleet no doubt.

Prices current. Four pounds a week for board,
besides finding your own washing, shaving, candles,
liquors, pipes, tobacco, wood, &c. Thirty shillings a
week for a servant. It ought to be thirty shillings for
a gentleman and four pounds for the servant, because
he generally eats twice as much, and makes twice as
much trouble. Shoes, five dollars a pair. Salt,
twenty-seven dollars a bushel. Butter, ten shillings
a pound. Punch, twenty shillings a bowl. All the
old women and young children are gone down to the
Jersey shore to make salt. Salt water is boiling all
round the coast, and I hope it will increase. For it is
nothing but heedlessness and shiftlessness that prevents us from making salt enough for a supply. But
necessity will bring us to it. As to sugar, molasses,
rum, &c., we must leave them off. Whiskey is used
here instead of rum, and I don't see but it is just as
good. Of this, the wheat and rye countries can easily
distil enough for the use of the country. If I could get
cider I would be content.

The business of the country has been in so critical
and dangerous a situation for the last twelve months,
that it was necessary the Massachusetts should have a
full representation, but the expenses of living are
grown so enormous that I believe it will be necessary
to reduce the number of Delegates to three, after the
campaign is over.

LETTER CXXXVIII.

Philadelphia, Saturday, 30 August, 1777.

MY FRIEND,

A LETTER from General Washington was received last night by the President, which I read. It is dated the 29th; yesterday.

The enemy are in possession of the Head of Elk, a little town at the head of the river Elk, in which they found a quantity of corn and oats belonging to the States. Waggons were so universally taken up in conveying away the valuable effects of the inhabitants, ·that none could be procured to transport this grain. Part of their army has advanced to Gray's hill, about two miles from the Head of Elk, but whether to take post there, or only to cover while they remove their plunder from the Head of Elk, is uncertain.

Our army is at Wilmington. We have many officers out reconnoitring the country and the enemy. Our scouting parties have taken between thirty and forty prisoners, and twelve deserters are come in from the fleet, and eight from the army. They say the men are generally healthy, but their horses have suffered much from the voyage. These prisoners and deserters are unable to give any other intelligence. The enemy give out that they are eighteen thousand strong. But these are like Burgoyne's, " make believes " and " insinuations." We know better ; and that they have not ten thousand. The militia from four States are joining General Washington in large numbers. The plan of their military operations this campaign is well calculated for our advantage. I hope we shall have heads and hearts to improve it.

For my own part I feel a secret wish that they might get into this city, because I think it more for our interest that they should be cooped up here, than that they should run away again to New York. But according to present appearances they will not be able to get here. By going into the Chesapeake bay, they have betrayed a dread of the fire works in the river Delaware, which indeed are formidable. They must make the most of their time, for they cannot rationally depend upon so fine a season late in the fall and early in winter as they had the last year. September, October and November are all that remain.

We expect hourly, advices from Gates and Arnold. We have rumors of an expedition to Long Island under Parsons, and another to Staten Island under Sullivan, but no regular accounts. I suppose it certain that such expeditions have been made, but know not the success.

Philadelphia, Monday, 1 September, 1777.

MY DEAR,

WE have now run through the summer, and although
the weather is still warm, the fiercest of the heat is
over. And although the extreme intemperance of
the late season has weakened and exhausted me much,
yet I think, upon the whole, I have got through it as
well as upon any former occasion.

A letter from General Washington, dated Saturday,
informs that our light parties have brought in four-and-
twenty prisoners more. So that the prisoners and deserters since Mr. Howe landed are near a hundred.
The question now is, whether there will be a general
engagement ? In the first place, I think, after all that
has passed, it is not good policy for us to attack them,
unless we can get a favorable advantage of them in
the situation of the ground, or an opportunity to attack a detachment of their army with superior numbers. It would be imprudent, perhaps, for us with our
whole force to attack them with all theirs.

But another question arises, whether Mr. Howe will
not be able to compel us to a general engagement ?
Perhaps he may ; but I make a question of it. Washington will manœuvre it with him a good deal to avoid
it. A general engagement, in which Howe should be
defeated, would be ruin to him. If we should be de-

feated, his army would be crippled, and perhaps we might suddenly reinforce our army, which he could not. However, all that he could gain by a victory would be the possession of this town, which would be the worst situation he could be in, because it would employ his whole force by sea and land to keep it and the command of the river.

Their principal dependence is not upon their arms, I believe, so much as upon the failure of our revenue. They think they have taken such measures, by circulating counterfeit bills, to depreciate the currency, that it cannot hold its credit longer than this campaign. But they are mistaken.

We, however, must disappoint them by renouncing all luxuries, and by a severe economy. General Washington sets a fine example. He has banished wine from his table, and entertains his friends with rum and water. This is much to the honor of his wisdom, his policy, and his patriotism. And the example must be followed by banishing sugar and all imported articles from our families. If necessity should reduce us to a simplicity of dress and diet becoming republicans, it would be a happy and a glorious necessity.

Yours, yours, yours.

Philadelphia, Tuesday, 2 September, 1777.

MY DEAR FRIEND,

I HAD, yesterday, the pleasure of yours of ——— , from Boston, and am happy to find that you have been able to do so well amidst all your difficulties. There is but one course for us to take, and that is to renounce the use of all foreign commodities. For my own part, I never lived in my whole life so meanly and poorly as I do now, and yet my constituents will growl at my extravagance. Happy should I be indeed, if I could share with you in the produce of your little farm. Milk, and apples, and pork, and beef, and the fruits of the garden would be luxury to me.

We had nothing yesterday from the General. Howe's army are in a very unwholesome situation. Their water is very bad and brackish. There are frequent morning and evening fogs, which produce intermittent fevers in abundance. Washington has a great body of militia assembled and assembling, in addition to a grand continental army. Whether he will strike or not, I can 't say. He is very prudent, you know, and will not unnecessarily hazard his army. By my own inward feelings, I judge, I should put more to risk if I were in his shoes, but perhaps he is right. Gansevoort has proved that it is possible to hold a post. Herkimer has shown that it is possible

to fight Indians, and Stark has proved that it is practicable even to attack lines and posts with militia. I
wish the continental army would prove that any thing
can be done. But this is sedition at least. I am
weary, however, I own, with so much insipidity.

St. Leger and his party have run away. So will
Burgoyne. I wish Stark had the supreme command
in the northern department. I am sick of Fabian
systems in all quarters. The officers drink a long and
moderate war. My toast is, a short and violent war.
They would call me mad and rash, &c., but I know
better. I am as cool as any of them, and cooler too,
for my mind is not inflamed with fear nor anger,
whereas, I believe theirs are with both. If this letter
should be intercepted and published, it would do as
much good as another did two years ago.

Adieu.

APPENDIX.

A.

INTERCEPTED LETTTERS. p. 57.

Two private and confidential letters written by John Adams, in the year 1775, which were intercepted and published by the British, are so frequently alluded to in this correspondence that it may not be unadvisable to give in this place some explanation of their history. The originals were taken in crossing the ferry at Newport, were sent on board the fleet of Admiral Graves, from thence fell into the hands of General Gage, and were by him transmitted to the Government at home. They are now in the State Paper Office in London. Copies were procured by some friend of his for Mr. Adams, from which they are now printed. The first of them was directed

"To the Honorable James Warren, Esquire at Watertown, by Mr. Hichbourne." This gentleman was then President of the provincial Congress of Massachusetts. It is as follows:

Philadelphia, 24 July, 1775.

DEAR SIR,

I am determined to write freely to you this time. A certain great fortune and piddling genius, whose fame has been trumpeted so loudly, has given a silly cast to our whole doings. We are between Hawk and Buzzard. We ought to have had in our hands, a month ago, the whole legislative, executive and judicial of the whole continent, and have completely modelled a constitution; to have raised a naval power and opened all our ports wide; to have arrested every friend of government on the continent and held them as hostages for the poor victims in Boston, and then opened the door as wide as possible for peace and reconciliation. After this, they might have petitioned, negotiated, addressed, &c., if they would. Is all this extravagant? Is it wild? Is it not the soundest policy? One piece of news, seven thousand pounds of powder arrived last night. We shall send you some of it as soon as we can, but you must be patient and frugal. We are lost in the extensiveness of our field of business. We have a continental treasury to establish, a paymaster to choose, and a committee of correspondence, or safety, or accounts, or something, I know not what, that has confounded us all this day.

Shall I hail you Speaker of the House, or councillor or what? What kind of an election had you? What sort of magistrates do you intend to make? Will your new legislative or executive feel bold or irresolute? Will your judicial hang, and whip, and fine, and imprison without scruple? I want to see our distressed country once more, yet I dread the sight of devastation. You observe in your letter the oddity of a great man. He is a queer creature, but you must love his dogs if you love him, and forgive a thousand whims for the sake of the soldier and the scholar.

Yours.

The other letter was directed "To Mrs. Abigail Adams, at Braintree, to the care of Colonel Warren, by Mr. Hichbourne," and runs as follows :

MY DEAR,

It is now almost three months since I left you, in every part of which, my anxiety about you and the children, as well as our country, has been extreme. The business I have had upon my mind has been as great and important as can be entrusted to man, and the difficulty and intricacy of it prodigious. When fifty or sixty men have a constitution to form for a great empire, at the same time that they have a country of fifteen hundred miles extent to fortify, millions to arm and train, a naval power to begin, an extensive commerce to regulate, numerous tribes of Indians to negotiate with, a standing army of twenty-seven thousand men to raise, pay, victual and officer, I really shall pity those fifty or sixty men. I must see you ere long. Rice has written me a very good letter. So has Thaxter, for which I thank them both. Love to the children.

J. A.

P. S. I wish I had given you a complete history, from the beginning to the end of the journey, of the behavior of my compatriots. No mortal tale can equal it. I will tell you in future, but you shall keep it secret. The fidgets, the whims, the caprice, the vanity, the superstition, the irritability of some of us is enough to —

Yours.

It frequently happens that papers excite public attention in a most extraordinary degree, not simply from the
matter which they contain, but also from the precise moment at which they make their appearance. Had these
letters been made public one year after the time they
were taken, so familiar had the sentiments which they
express then become, that they would have excited little
notice. As it was, there is abundant evidence, without
resorting to the present collection, of the great effect
which they produced, both in Great Britain and America.
The second petition to the King had been drawn up and
carried through Congress by Mr. John Dickinson, against
all the efforts which Mr. Adams could make in opposition, two weeks before the date of these letters. He was
" the great fortune and piddling genius," who is alluded
to at the commencement of the first one. This endeavor to
procure the adoption of a second measure of conciliation,
after the failure of the first, was regarded by Mr. Adams as a
backward step in the course of events that was impelling the
country to assume independence of Great Britain, and was
for that reason most strenuously but unavailingly resisted by
him. His mind, which had always been in advance of public sentiment, was rapidly maturing all the organization
that was necessarily to follow the Declaration, long before those of his fellow citizens generally had become prepared even to take that step itself. The details of this organization are sketched in these two letters, and constitute
all that is remarkable about them. Neither the ministry
at home nor the public mind out of New England had
been at all prepared beforehand to receive them. The
consequence was, that Mr. Adams was by their publication placed in an extremely difficult and exposed situation.
Governor Gage enclosed them in a letter to Lord Dart-
mouth, and most erroneously endeavored to prove from
them the existence of a scheme of rebellion preconcerted

years before in Massachusetts.[1] The ministry probably received them at about the same time with the second petition to the King, and very naturally inferred from
them a want of sincerity on the part of the Congress
which was not founded in justice. For in fact there had
been an opposition of opinion in that body, in which the
minority had yielded without being convinced, and Mr.
Adams only represented that minority.

In the letter of Mrs. Adams of the 2 — 10 March, 1776,
she mentions a cousin who " writes from England that
these letters have made much noise there," and laments
that Mr. Adams ever wrote them. This was the natural
course of a person of limited views surrounded by Englishmen friendly to America, and still clinging to the
hope of reconciliation. Mr. Adams must have appeared
to such men as exposing himself to just censure, although
he was only marking out, in broad lines, the foundations for
a system of government which, he foresaw though they
could not, must be a necessary consequence of the measures originated and persevered in by the mother country
itself; measures, which he did not suppose would ever
be abandoned, however others might flatter themselves
that they would. It was the proof first presented to the
eyes of the British, in these letters, that the remonstrants
were fully capable of a sustained policy, and that the resistance to them was something more than momentary
impulse, which gave to them such importance in their
eyes. The general tone of the English, particularly of
the regular army, towards the colonists, had always been
one of sovereign contempt. Hence the mode in which
these letters were received by the garrison in Boston, was
that of ridicule. The importance attached by Mr. Ad-

[1] " The Writings of Washington," edited by Mr. Jared
Sparks, Vol. ii. 499, Vol. iii. 514.

ams to the measures of the Congress, was regarded
as ludicrously self-sufficient and absurd. The officers
amused themselves in making paraphrases. One of
these is referred to in Mrs. Adams's letter of the 22d of
October of this year, in which she says that they inserted
as much of scurrility against the author as they could
frame out of the details of his life.

But all this, however much of relaxation it may have
afforded to idlers in the British ranks, was productive of no
inconvenience whatever to Mr. Adams himself. The same
thing cannot be said of the effect which the publication of
the letters had upon him when they reached Philadelphia.
They contained indirect censure of a majority of the Congress who had chosen to follow Mr. Dickinson's lead, as
well as a reflection upon that gentleman himself, and
upon the humors of some of his own colleagues. They
also contained a notice not altogether complimentary of
General Charles Lee. The persons thus commented upon
were probably not unwilling to give vent to their private
griefs by falling into the current of indignation which immediately set against Mr. Adams's doctrines upon public affairs. The consequence was, that he fell under a
sentence of almost total excommunication. Many of
his subsequent letters throughout this volume, contain
allusions to the consequences of this event to him, and it
appears to have made him for a long time more cautious
in expressing himself. In a character of Mr. Adams,
drawn by Dr. Benjamin Rush, and now in manuscript in
the hands of the Editor of these letters, it is stated that
these letters "exposed him to the execrations of all the
prudent and moderate people in America, insomuch that
he was treated with neglect by many of his old friends."
"I saw," he proceeds, "this gentleman walk the streets of
Philadelphia, alone, after the publication of his intercepted
letter in our newspapers in 1775, an object of nearly uni-

versal scorn and detestation. Events soon justified the wish contained in his letter, after which he rose in the public estimation so as to become in the subsequent years of the revolution, in some measure the oracle of the Whigs." The lapse of little more than twelve months found Mr. Adams and Mr. Dickinson in a position completely reversed, the latter gentleman complaining of a desertion much the same in character with that which had happened to the former. Such, it may be remarked, is the usual fate of men engaged in contests with each other upon great public questions, where the indiscreet sagacity of one party runs almost as far in advance of the popular opinion as the prudent timidity of the other keep it following in the rear.

B.   p. 235.

THOUGHTS ON GOVERNMENT.

The following memorandum was found among the papers of Mr. Adams, written upon a single leaf which appears once to have preceded a copy of the letter to George Wythe.

In the winter of 1776 there was much discussion in Congress concerning the necessity of independence, and advising the several States to institute governments for themselves under the immediate authority and original power of the people. Great difficulties occurred to many gentlemen in making a transition from the old governments to new, i. e., from the royal to republican governments. In January, 1776, Mr. George Wythe of Virginia, passing an evening with me, asked what plan I would advise a colony to pursue, in order to get out of the old government and into a new one. I sketched in words a scheme, which he requested me to give him in writing. Accordingly, the next day, I delivered to him the following letter. He lent it to his colleague, Richard Henry Lee, who asked me to let him print it; to which I consented, provided he would suppress my name; for if that should appear, it would excite a continental clamor among the Tories, that I was erecting a battering ram to demolish the royal government and render independence indispensable.

QUINCY, 21 July, 1811.

The copy of the letter to which this notice was prefixed, is now separated from it, and neither that nor any other has been discovered among the papers. Judge Cranch, when preparing his Memoir of Mr. Adams for the Columbian Institute at Washington, was unable to find it in print, notwithstanding that it has been several times published; once anonymously by Dunlap in Philadelphia, at the time it was written; once by Thomas in the Massachusetts Spy, by whom it was attributed to Mr. Jefferson; and once more with the author's name, that of the person to whom it was addressed, and with the preceding preface. It is now taken from the Appendix to the Memoir of John Adams in the " Biography of the Signers to the Declaration of Independence," published by Sanderson, in Philadelphia. Another letter is to be found in a volume entitled " An inquiry into the principles and policy of the government of the United States, by John Taylor of Caroline county, Virginia," so closely resembling it in language and substance, that it was considered by Mr. Taylor at the time to be the same. But the publication elicited from Mr. Adams, in a private letter to him, an explanation, which, as connected with the history of the period, although perhaps, at the hazard of a little repetition, is here subjoined.

"I suspect, by some accident or other, you have confounded together a little printed pamphlet with a letter that was never printed. Let me give you an unvarnished explanation according to my best recollection. In January, 1776, six months before the Declaration of Independence, Mr. Wythe, of Virginia, passed an evening with me at my chamber. In the course of conversation upon the necessity of independence, Mr. Wythe observing that the greatest obstacle in the way of a declaration of it was the difficulty of agreeing upon a government for our future regulation; I replied, that each colony should form a government for itself, as a free and independent state. " Well," said Mr. Wythe, " what plan would you institute or advise for any one of the States?" My answer was, " It is a thing I have not thought much of, but I will give you the first ideas that occur to me ;" and I went on to explain to him, off hand and in short hand, my first thoughts. Mr. Wythe appeared to think more of them than I did, and requested me to put down in writing what I had then said. I agreed, and accordingly that night and the next morning, wrote it and sent it in a letter to him. This letter he sent to R. H. Lee, who came and asked my leave to print it. I said it was not fit to be printed, nor worth printing, but if he thought otherwise, he might, provided he would suppress my name. He went accordingly to Dunlap and had it printed under the title of " Thoughts on government, in a letter from a gentleman to his friend." Thus much for the printed pamphlet. Now for the unprinted letter. Some time in the ensuing spring the delegates from North Carolina called upon me with a vote of the legislature of their State instructing them to apply to me for advice concerning a form of government to be instituted in that State. I blushed, to be sure, to find that my name had reached so far as North Carolina, and still more at such an unexpected honor from so respectable an assembly. Overwhelmed, however, as I was at that period, night and day, with business in Congress and on committees, I found moments to write a letter, perhaps as long as that to Mr. Wythe, and containing nearly the same outlines. In what points the two letters agree or differ I know not, for I kept no copy and have never seen it or heard of it since, till your volume revived the recollection of it."

THOUGHTS ON GOVERNMENT, IN A LETTER FROM A GENTLE-
MAN TO HIS FRIEND.

MY DEAR SIR,

IF I was equal to the task of forming a plan for the government of a colony, I should be flattered with your request, and very happy to comply with it; because as the divine science of politics is the science of social happiness, and the blessings of society depend entirely on the constitutions of government, which are generally institutions that last for many generations, there can be no employment more agreeable to a benevolent mind, than a research after the best.

Pope flattered tyrants too much when he said,

> " For forms of government let fools contest,
> " That which is best administered is best."

Nothing can be more fallacious than this: But poets read history to collect flowers, not fruits; they attend to fanciful images, not the effects of social institutions. Nothing is more certain from the history of nations, and nature of man, than that some forms of government are better fitted for being well administered than others.

We ought to consider what is the end of government, before we determine which is the best form. Upon this point all speculative politicians will agree, that the happiness of society is the end of government, as all divines and moral philosophers will agree that the happiness of the individual is the end of man. From this principle it will follow, that the form of government, which communicates ease, comfort, security, or in one word happiness, to the greatest number of persons, and in the greatest degree, is the best.

All sober inquirers after truth, ancient and modern, pagan and Christian, have declared that the happiness of man, as well as his dignity, consists in virtue. Confucius, Zoroaster, Socrates, Mahomet, not to mention authorities really sacred, have agreed in this.

If there is a form of government then, whose principle and foundation is virtue, will not every sober man acknowledge it better calculated to promote the general happiness than any other form ?

Fear is the foundation of most governments; but it is so sordid and brutal a passion, and renders men, in whose breasts it predominates, so stupid and miserable, that Americans will not be likely to approve of any political institution which is founded on it.

Honor is truly sacred, but holds a lower rank in the scale of moral excellence than virtue. Indeed the former is but a part of the latter, and consequently has not equal pretensions to support a frame of government productive of human happiness.

The foundation of every government is some principle or passion in the minds of the people. The noblest principles and most generous affections in our nature then, have the fairest chance to support the noblest and most generous models of government.

A man must be indifferent to the sneers of modern Englishmen, to mention in their company, the names of Sidney, Harrington, Locke, Milton, Nedham, Neville, Burnet and Hoadley. No small fortitude is necessary to confess that one has read them. The wretched condition of this country, however, for ten or fifteen years past, has frequently reminded me of their principles and reasonings. They will convince any candid mind, that there is no good government but what is republican. That the only valuable part of the British constitution is so; because the very definition of a republic, is "an empire of laws, and not of men." That, as a republic is the best of governments, so that particular arrangement of the powers of society, or in other words that form of government, which is best contrived to secure an impartial and exact execution of the laws, is the best of republics.

Of republics, there is an inexhaustible variety, because the possible combinations of the powers of society, are capable of innumerable variations.

As good government, is an empire of laws, how shall your laws be made? In a large society, inhabiting an extensive country, it is impossible that the whole should assemble to make laws. The first necessary step then, is, to depute power from the many, to a few of the most wise and good. But by what rules shall you choose your representatives? Agree upon the number and qualifications of persons, who shall have the benefit of choosing, or annex this privilege to the inhabitants of a certain extent of ground.

The principal difficulty lies, and the greatest care should be employed in constituting this representative assembly. It should be in miniature an exact portrait of the people at large. It should think, feel, reason and act like them. That it may be the interest of this assembly to do strict justice at all times, it should be an equal representation, or in other words equal interest among the people should have equal interest in it. Great care should be taken to effect this, and to prevent unfair, partial, and corrupt elections. Such regulations, however, may be better made in times of greater tranquillity than the present, and they will spring up themselves naturally, when all the powers of government come to be in the hands of the people's friends. At present it will be safest to proceed in all established modes, to which the people have been familiarized by habit.

A representation of the people in one assembly being obtained, a question arises whether all the powers of government, legislative, executive, and judicial, shall be left in this body? I think a people cannot be long free, nor ever happy, whose government is in one assembly. My reasons for this opinion are as follow:

1. A single assembly is liable to all the vices, follies and frailties of an individual; subject to fits of humor, starts of passion, flights of enthusiasm, partialities or prejudice, and consequently productive of hasty results and absurd judgments. And all these errors ought to be corrected and defects supplied by some controlling power.

2. A single assembly is apt to be avaricious, and in time will not scruple to exempt itself from burdens which it will lay, without compunction, on its constituents.

3. A single assembly is apt to grow ambitious, and after a time will not hesitate to vote itself perpetual. This was one fault of the long parliament, but more remarkably of Holland, whose assembly first voted themselves from annual to septennial, then for life, and after a course of years, that all vacancies happening by death or otherwise

should be filled by themselves, without any application to constituents at all.

4. A representative assembly, although extremely well qualified, and absolutely necessary as a branch of the legislative, is unfit to exercise the executive power, for want of two essential properties, secrecy and despatch.

5. A representative assembly is still less qualified for the judicial power; because it is too numerous, too slow, and too little skilled in the laws.

6. Because a single assembly possessed of all the powers of government, would make arbitrary laws for their own interest, execute all laws arbitrarily for their own interest, and adjudge all controversies in their own favor.

But shall the whole power of legislation rest in one assembly? Most of the foregoing reasons apply equally to prove that the legislative power ought to be more complex — to which we may add, that if the legislative power is wholly in one assembly, and the executive in another, or in a single person, these two powers will oppose and encroach upon each other, until the contest shall end in war, and the whole power, legislative and executive, be usurped by the strongest.

The judicial power, in such case, could not mediate, or hold the balance between the two contending powers, because the legislative would undermine it. And this shows the necessity too, of giving the executive power a negative upon the legislative, otherwise this will be continually encroaching upon that.

To avoid these dangers let a distinct assembly be constituted, as a mediator between the two extreme branches of the legislature, that which represents the people and that which is vested with the executive power.

Let the representative assembly then elect by ballot, from among themselves or their constituents, or both, a distinct assembly, which for the sake of perspicuity we will call a council. It may consist of any number you please, say twenty or thirty, and should have a free and independent exercise of its judgment, and consequently a negative voice in the legislature.

These two bodies thus constituted, and made integral parts of the legislature, let them unite, and by joint ballot choose a governor, who, after being stripped of most of those badges of domination called prerogatives, should have a free and independent exercise of his judgment, and be made also an integral part of the legislature. This I know is liable to objections, and if you please you may make him only president of the council, as in Connecticut: But as the governor is to be invested with the executive power, with consent of council, I think he ought to have a negative upon the legislative. If he is annually elective, as he ought to be, he will always have so much reverence and affection for the people, their representatives and councillors, that although you give him an independent exercise of his judgment, he will seldom use it in opposition to the two houses, except in cases the public utility of which would be conspicuous; and some such cases would happen.

In the present exigency of American affairs, when by an act of parliament we are put out of the royal protection, and consequently discharged from our allegiance; and it has become necessary to assume government for our immediate security, the governor, lieutenant governor, secretary, treasurer, commissary, attorney-general, should be chosen by joint ballot, of both houses. And these and all other elections, especially of representatives and councillors, should be annual, there not being in the whole circle of the sciences, a maxim more infallible than this, " where annual elections end, there slavery begins."

These great men, in this respect, should be, once a year,

> " Like bubbles on the sea of matter borne,
> " They rise, they break, and to that sea return."

This will teach them the great political virtues of humility, patience, and moderation, without which every man in power becomes a ravenous beast of prey.

This mode of constituting the great offices of state will answer very well for the present, but if, by experiment, it should be found inconvenient, the legislature may at its leisure devise other methods of creating them, by elections of the people at large, as in Connecticut, or it may enlarge the term for which they shall be chosen to seven years, or three years, or for life, or make any other alterations which the society shall find productive of its ease, its safety, its freedom, or in one word its happiness.

A rotation of all offices, as well as of representatives and councillors, has many advocates, and is contended for with many plausible arguments. It would be attended no doubt with many advantages, and if the society has a sufficient number of suitable characters to supply the great number of vacancies which would be made by such a rotation, I can see no objection to it. These persons may be allowed to serve for three years, and then be excluded three years, or for any longer or shorter term.

Any seven or nine of the legislative council may be made a quorum, for doing business as a privy council, to advise the governor in the exercise of the executive branch of power, and in all acts of state.

The governor should have the command of the militia, and of all your armies. The power of pardons should be with the governor and council.

Judges, justices and all other officers, civil and military, should be nominated and appointed by the governor, with the advice and consent of council, unless you choose to have a government more popular; if you do, all officers, civil and military, may be chosen by joint ballot, of both houses, or in order to preserve the independence and importance of each house, by ballot of one house, concurred in by the other. Sheriffs should be chosen by the freeholders of counties — so should registers of deeds and clerks of counties.

All officers should have commissions, under the hand of the governor and seal of the colony.

The dignity and stability of government in all its branches, the morals of the people and every blessing of society, depend so much upon an upright and skilful administration of justice, that the judicial power ought to be distinct from both the legislative and executive, and independent upon both, that so it may be a check upon both, as both should be checks upon that. The judges therefore should always be men of learning and experience in the laws, of exemplary morals, great patience, calmness, coolness and attention. Their minds should not be distracted with jarring interests; they should not be dependent upon any man, or body of men. To these ends they should hold estates for life in their offices, or in other words their commissions should be during good behavior, and their salaries ascertained and established by law. For misbehavior the grand inquest of the colony, the house of representatives, should impeach them before the governor and council, where they should have time and opportunity to make their defence, but if convicted should be removed from their offices, and subjected to such other punishment as shall be thought proper.

A militia law requiring all men, or with very few exceptions besides cases of conscience, to be provided with arms and ammunition, to be trained at certain seasons; and

requiring counties, towns, or other small districts to be
provided with public stocks of ammunition and intrench-
ing utensils, and with some settled plans for transporting
provisions after the militia, when marched to defend their
country against sudden invasions; and requiring certain
districts to be provided with field-pieces, companies of
matrosses, and perhaps some regiments of light horse, is
always a wise institution, and in the present circumstances of our country indispensable.

Laws for the liberal education of youth, especially of
the lower class of people, are so extremely wise and useful, that to a humane and generous mind, no expense for
this purpose would be thought extravagant.

The very mention of sumptuary laws will excite a
smile. Whether our countrymen have wisdom and virtue enough to submit to them I know not. But the happiness of the people might be greatly promoted by them,
and a revenue saved sufficient to carry on this war forever. Frugality is a great revenue, besides curing us of
vanities, levities and fopperies which are real antidotes
to all great, manly and warlike virtues.

But must not all commissions run in the name of a
king? No. Why may they not as well run thus, " The
colony of   to A. B. greeting," and be tested by the
governor?

Why may not writs, instead of running in the name of
the king, run thus, " the colony of   to the sheriff,"
&c. and be tested by the chief justice ?

Why may not indictments conclude " against the peace
of the colony of   and the dignity of the same ? "

A constitution, founded on these principles, introduces
knowledge among the people, and inspires them with a
conscious dignity, becoming freemen. A general emulation takes place, which causes good humor, sociability,
good manners, and good morals to be general. That ele-

vation of sentiment inspired by such a government, makes the common people brave and enterprising. That ambition which is inspired by it makes them sober, industrious and frugal. You will find among them some elegance, perhaps, but more solidity; a little pleasure, but a great deal of business; some politeness, but more civility. If you compare such a country with the regions of domination, whether monarchical or aristocratical, you will fancy yourself in Arcadia or Elisium.

If the colonies should assume governments separately, they should be left entirely to their own choice of the forms, and if a continental constitution should be formed, it should be a congress, containing a fair and adequate representation of the colonies, and its authority should sacredly be confined to these cases, viz. war, trade, disputes between colony and colony, the post office, and the unappropriated lands of the crown, as they used to be called.

These colonies, under such forms of government, and in such a union, would be unconquerable by all the monarchies of Europe.

You and I, my dear friend, have been sent into life, at a time when the greatest lawgivers of antiquity would have wished to live. How few of the human race have ever enjoyed an opportunity of making an election of government more than of air, soil or climate, for themselves or their children! When before the present epocha, had three millions of people full power and a fair opportunity to form and establish the wisest and happiest government that human wisdom can contrive? I hope you will avail yourself and your country of that extensive learning and indefatigable industry which you possess, to assist her in the formation of the happiest governments, and the best character of a great people. For myself, I must beg you to keep my name out of sight, for this feeble attempt, if it should be known to be mine, would oblige me to apply to myself those lines of the immortal John Milton, in one of his sonnets,

> " I did but prompt the age to quit their clogs
> " By the known rules of ancient liberty,
> " When strait a barbarous noise environs me,
> " Of owls and cuckoos, asses, apes and dogs."

END OF VOL. I.

For EU product safety concerns, contact us at Calle de José Abascal, 56–1°,
28003 Madrid, Spain or eugpsr@cambridge.org.

www.ingramcontent.com/pod-product-compliance
Ingram Content Group UK Ltd.
Pitfield, Milton Keynes, MK11 3LW, UK
UKHW040617240426
470322UK00010B/174